AIR CAMPAIGN

NEW GUINEA 1943–44

The Allies assume the offensive

JOHN ROGERS & MARK STILLE | ILLUSTRATED BY JIM LAURIER

OSPREY PUBLISHING
Bloomsbury Publishing Plc
Kemp House, Chawley Park, Cumnor Hill, Oxford OX2 9PH, UK
Bloomsbury Publishing Ireland Limited,
29 Earlsfort Terrace, Dublin 2, D02 AY28, Ireland
1359 Broadway, 12th Floor, New York, NY 10018, USA
E-mail: info@ospreypublishing.com
www.ospreypublishing.com

OSPREY is a trademark of Osprey Publishing Ltd

First published in Great Britain in 2026

A catalog record for this book is available from the British Library.

ISBN: PB 9781472870353; eBook 9781472870360; ePDF 9781472870377; XML 9781472870346

26 27 28 29 30 10 9 8 7 6 5 4 3 2 1

Maps by www.bounford.com
3D BEV by Paul Kime
Index by Alan Rutter
Typeset by Lumina Datamatics Ltd
Printed by Repro India Ltd.

Title page: see p.65.

MIX Paper FSC FSC® C047271

Osprey Publishing supports the Woodland Trust, the UK's leading woodland conservation charity.

CONTENTS

INTRODUCTION

From early 1943, the B-24 was the workhorse of Kenney's heavy bomber force. It featured a long range and large bomb load and could be modified to conduct a variety of missions. This 321st Bomb Squadron B-24D, modified with a nose turret, heads for Wewak probably on February 3, 1944. (NARA)

The Allies had by May 1943 wrested the strategic initiative from the Japanese in New Guinea. Gen. Douglas MacArthur, Supreme Commander of the Allied Forces, Southwest Pacific Area (SWPA), was granted strategic authority over Adm. William Halsey's South Pacific (SOPAC) theater to coordinate plans and operations. MacArthur's Operation *Cartwheel* outlined efforts by SWPA and SOPAC against the major Japanese air and naval base at Rabaul on New Britain. MacArthur's *Elkton III* plan, the SWPA portion of *Cartwheel*, laid out a series of operations for seizing control of the straits between New Guinea and New Britain during 1943.

These objectives were in line with MacArthur's long-term desire to press forward with the capture of New Guinea in preparation for retaking the Philippines. Air power would be vital to accomplish MacArthur's ambition. Lt Gen. George C. Kenney, MacArthur's Allied Air Forces commander, had engineered a winning strategy in 1942 employing the limited resources of the United States Army Air Force (USAAF) 5th Air Force and the Royal Australian Air Force (RAAF) Command to stop the Japanese takeover of New Guinea. MacArthur then called upon Kenney to devise the plans and methods to facilitate the Allied conquest of the whole of New Guinea.

This was a tall order inasmuch as the Combined Chiefs of Staff's (CCS) (comprised of the American and British joint chiefs of staffs) priority of defeating Germany first limited the personnel and equipment available for the SWPA campaign, and unfavorable conditions in New Guinea – terrain, weather, distance, and environment – that the Allies had struggled mightily with during 1942 still remained. Kenney and his key subordinates realized that enhanced operational flexibility would be even more necessary to get the maximum use out of what resources the Allied Air Forces did possess. Building on command, weaponeering, and tactical innovations, Kenney selected capable subordinates and gave them a relatively free hand in supporting MacArthur's campaign while tirelessly coaxing additional men and planes out of the Joint Chiefs of Staff (JCS) and ensuring adequate maintenance and training for them to carry the fight to the Japanese.

For the Japanese, the slow but steady growth in Allied air power, and the gains in both New Guinea and the Solomons this growth enabled, forced their Imperial General Headquarters (IGHQ) to revise its earlier expansive strategy to one of establishing a defensive perimeter that could realistically be held, given the resources available for the South Pacific. Since the Imperial Japanese Navy (IJN) and the Imperial Japanese Army (IJA) did not enjoy a cooperative relationship, rather functioning as antagonistic entities with different strategic objectives and operational outlooks, the formulation and execution of this revised strategy was muddled and incomplete. Their commitment and use of air power to defend Japanese positions in New Guinea and the Solomons suffered greatly from this strategic confusion. This situation ultimately resulted, in the case of New Guinea, in their utter inability to halt, or even significantly impede, the series of Allied offensive moves that saw the destruction or entrapment of significant IJA forces in New Guinea by July 1944.

The frequent bad weather affected both sides to a significant degree. Clouds and storm fronts often caused poor results during missions or prohibited flying altogether. It also slowed airfield construction work and aircraft maintenance that often took place in the open. Here No 76 Squadron personnel take shelter from the rain at Kiriwina. (AWM)

The antagonists fought the campaign under the most difficult conditions imaginable. They were subject to the same two complicating, and interrelated, situational factors: the distances and the environment of the battlespace. In the case of distances, the campaign the Allies fought covered about 1,500 miles along the main axis of effort, the northern New Guinea coast. For Allied units flying from the North-Western Area (NWA), many critical targets for tying down or deflecting Japanese air and maritime reinforcements for New Guinea were 1,000 miles or more distant. The Japanese transit route for aircraft ran from Formosa to New Guinea with several intermediate stages. Both sides were also handicapped by the relatively short time their fighters could escort land-based bombers and engage enemy fighters. Even with the antagonists later building several staging/recovery airfields as the campaign progressed, physical distances were a constant challenge to air operations.

As for the environment, both sides were adversely affected by the weather and the dense jungle terrain. The entire region was susceptible to major fluctuations in cloud density and altitude, and tropical storm fronts formed quickly; sustained heavy rains were frequent. Additionally, accurate weather forecasting was almost impossible. All this often made navigating long distances to targets impossible or at least extremely difficult. Targets were often obscured by the time they were reached. On the ground, the foul weather made maintenance on and movement of aircraft very difficult at airfields with poor drainage and few or no permanent shelters and created breeding grounds for insects carrying debilitating diseases such as malaria, scrub typhus, and dengue fever that severely afflicted personnel. The terrain on New Guinea also presented a major obstacle. The jungle covering New Guinea was in most areas virtually impenetrable and, along with shark-infested waters surrounding the island, greatly limited the chances of survival of pilots downed over land or water, as well as the combatants' ability to create and easily supply new airfields.

CHRONOLOGY

1943

May Allied reconnaissance locates a suitable spot, Tsili Tsili, to develop an airfield to bring fighters within range of Huon Peninsula objectives as well as Wewak-area targets.

May 14 First major air battle of the campaign sees American fighters beat off an IJNAF attack on an Allied convoy in Oro Bay.

June 5th Air Force receives its first full P-47 and P-38 fighter groups, enhancing its ability to escort bombers at greater distances and fully assume the offensive against the IJAAF in New Guinea.

June 6th Air Division launches attacks on various Allied airfields under construction in the New Guinea highlands.

June 30 Allies conduct amphibious seizures of Woodlark and Kiriwina Islands, and Nassau Bay on New Guinea's northeast coast southeast of Salamaua.

July 26 Tsili Tsili available for operations; 35th Fighter Group fully occupies it by late August.

August 10 4th Air Army establishes its headquarters at Wewak.

August 15 IJAAF mounts an attack against the Allied airbase at Tsili Tsili after discovering its presence the previous day.

August 17–18 5th Air Force offensive against Wewak-area targets commences.

September 4–5 Australians land at Hopoi, just east of Lae, and move west to capture Lae; US siezes Nadzab, later used as a jumping off point for Australians to assault on Lae from the west.

September 22 Australians land north of Finschhafen; they capture the airfield on October 2.

October 12–November 5 SWPA conducts daylight raids against Rabaul-area targets (SOPAC assumes responsibility for Rabaul thereafter).

November–December A series of IJAAF raids against Gusap and Nadzab fail to disrupt Allied operations from either location.

December Allied New Britain landings at Arawe on the 15th and Cape Gloucester on the 26th.

1944

January 2 Americans land at Saidor and begin improving airfield; both sides of Vitiaz–Dampier Straits occupied by the Allies.

January At meetings in Washington, Kenney secures JCS promises for new units, to include Thirteenth Air Force once Rabaul is neutralized.

February 3 Major USAAF attack on Wewak-area airfields leaves more than 50 IJAAF aircraft destroyed and preempts any major 4th Air Army operations.

February 29 Allies land at Los Negros in the Admiralty Islands and seize Momote airfield; all Japanese resistance in the Admiralties ends by March 25.

February–April Shift of most Allied air units forward to Gusap, Nadzab, and Saidor to prepare for the final phase of the campaign.

March 25 4th Air Army moves its headquarters to Hollandia.

March 30–April 3 A series of three attacks on Hollandia, Cyclops, and Sentani airfields almost annihilates 4th Air Army.

April 12 Massive daylight bombing raid on Hollandia, the key remaining Japanese base complex on New Guinea, devastates the town and support infrastructure.

April 13 IJNAF 23rd Air Flotilla moves its headquarters from Davao to Sorong, and its aircraft into several New Guinea airfields to bolster IJAAF elements still opposing the Allied advance.

April 15 4th Air Army moves headquarters to Menado in the Celebes, leaving 6th Air Division at Wewak to face the Allied onslaught.

To prepare for MacArthur's Hollandia assault, 5th Air Force attacked the town itself and military facilities at Humboldt Bay. With the bay in the background, a 64th Bomb Squadron B-24 heads home after dropping its portion of 322 tons of bombs on personnel/storage areas near Hollandia on April 12, 1944. (NARA)

April 16 5th Air Force records heavy losses in aircraft and aircrew on "Black Sunday" due to inclement weather following the day's missions; the worst day suffered by 5th Air Force during the campaign.

April 22 Double landings at Hollandia and at Aitape allow Allies to capture four airfields within days.

May 17–18 Americans land at Arare and seize Wakde airfield.

May 27 US forces land on Biak; fighting lasts until July, though the island's airfields are in use by late June; the smaller island of Owi also seized and an airfield built there is ready by mid-June.

June 15 Stand-up of Far East Air Forces (FEAF) under the command of Kenney, subsuming both 5th and 13th Air Forces.

July 2 Americans land at Noemfoor, and have control of island by July 6.

July 30–31 Seizure of Mar, Middleburg Island, and Cape Sansipor completes Allied amphibious operations on New Guinea.

ATTACKER'S CAPABILITIES

On June 15, 1944, Lt Gen. George C. Kenney (center) became commander of USAAF Far East Air Forces, and 13th Air Force joined 5th Air Force under Kenney. Maj. Gens. Ennis Whitehead (left) and St. Clair "Bill" Streett (right) assumed command of 5th and 13th Air Forces, respectively. (NARA)

Command organization and leadership

The Allied command structure in place since September 1942 was retained and refined as the Allies assumed the offensive in New Guinea. Headquartered in Brisbane, Kenney, as Commander, Allied Air Forces, held command of 5th Air Force directly and of RAAF Command through Air Vice-Marshal (AVM) William Bostock. On June 15, 1944, Kenney became head of FEAF. This USAAF organization fell under Allied Air Forces and included both 5th and 13th Air Forces, the latter having begun transferring from SOPAC in April 1944. Maj. Gen. Ennis C. Whitehead became 5th Air Force commander while Maj. Gen. St. Clair "Bill" Streett assumed command of 13th Air Force.

Administrative oversight of 5th Air Force combat units was the responsibility of V Bomber Command and V Fighter Command. Day-to-day operational authority over Allied air units was exercised by Kenney via the 5th Air Force Advanced Echelon (ADVON), headed by Whitehead. This entity, which Kenney created in Port Moresby in August 1942, did not fit within USAAF command and control doctrine, but it allowed more flexible operational tasking. An additional command innovation established by Kenney was the air task force. Nominally subordinate to ADVON and likewise not part of official USAAF doctrine, an air task force had air units assigned to it on an ad hoc basis (usually every unit based at a particular airfield) and would task missions to its units as specified by ADVON. A task force could also order missions on its own initiative if circumstances warranted. This entity was created in part to overcome endemic SWPA communications problems and proved very useful during the campaign as Allied air power grew and movement of units westward on an often accelerated timetable became commonplace. But since an air task force was not a formally recognized entity by USAAF headquarters in Washington DC, to get adequate staffing assigned through the US Army personnel system, the task forces were given the designations of the 308th Heavy (H), 309th (H), and 310th Medium (M) Bomb Wings in February 1944. The bomb wings continued to execute 5th Air Force orders after ADVON's disestablishment when FEAF was formed.

The First Air Task Force at Dobodura was headed by Brig. Gen. Frederic Smith, 5th Air Force Assistant Chief of Staff under Kenney. Later, additional air task forces were set up, usually as a major airbase was developed and occupied by various units. Thus, in October 1943, the Second Air Task Force stood up at Tsili Tsili and later moved to Nadzab, and the Third stood up at Gusap. In March 1944, RAAF Air Commodore (Air Cmdre) Frederick R.W. Scherger was put in charge of the air task force for the Aitape operation. Kenney named Streett Commander, 13th Task Force, which title he held during the 13th Air Force's transition from SOPAC to SWPA control between April and June 1944.

AVM William Bostock headed RAAF Command throughout the campaign. His running feud with Chief of the Air Staff, AVM Jones, caused much friction among senior personnel, but ultimately did not hinder RAAF operations. (NARA)

All RAAF and Royal Air Force (RAF) combat squadrons, the Dutch bomber squadron, and some USAAF heavy bomber squadrons were assigned to RAAF Command under Bostock, who had interwar experience on the RAF's Bomber Command staff and had also served as RAAF Deputy Chief of Staff with responsibility for operations and intelligence. The RAAF operational chain was further divided during the campaign among various areas, operational groups, and wings. All RAAF units fighting in New Guinea initially fell under No 9 Operational Group, headed from February 1943 by Air Cmdre Joseph E. Hewitt, who had been Kenney's Director for Intelligence at Allied Air Forces headquarters. He was succeeded by AVM Francis W.F. Lukis on December 18, 1943, under murky circumstances tied to intra-RAAF politics. In November 1943, No 10 Operational Group, headed by then-Gp Capt. Scherger, was formed at Nadzab as the campaign moved westward. The RAAF NWA, which had stood fast against Japanese encroachment from the Netherlands East Indies (NEI) since early 1942, controlled several fighter and bomber squadrons, and was commanded by Air Cmdre Francis M. Bladin until July 1943, then by AVM Adrian T. "King" Cole. Finally, the RAAF North-Eastern Area (NEA) commanded by AVM Arthur H. Cobby also had a very minor role in the campaign defending the Torres Strait and the Allied positions such as Merauke on New Guinea's southern coast from IJN predation.

RAAF Headquarters in Melbourne, headed by AVM George Jones, retained administrative control over all RAAF units, with responsibility to man, train, and equip squadrons. Junior in rank to Bostock, Jones was sensitive to real or perceived slights to his authority, which to him the very existence of RAAF Command under Bostock represented. During the campaign the RAAF senior leadership engaged in tense bureaucratic conflict pitting Bostock's pride against Jones' insecurities. This situation was known to and tolerated by MacArthur and Kenney because from their perspective there were no better alternatives to the existing RAAF organization and, in any case, RAAF operations were not negatively affected.

Aircraft

In May 1943 Kenney's 5th Air Force consisted of three heavy bomb groups, three medium bomb groups, two transport groups, a reconnaissance squadron, and three fighter groups. He also had a major airbase north of the daunting Owen Stanley Range at Dobodura with seaborne supply facilities nearby at Oro Bay. During and immediately after the Buna fighting, the Allied air units had almost all moved from Australia's NEA to New Guinea, mainly around Port Moresby and Milne Bay. This decreased the distances needed to reach Japanese targets on and north of New Guinea, which in turn decreased somewhat the wear and tear on Allied aircraft and aircrews.

Hewitt's No 9 Operational Group possessed three fighter squadrons, three light bomber squadrons, and two attack squadrons. Kenney, as Allied Air Forces commander, also had use of the resources assigned to the RAAF Command's NEA and NWA, headquartered at Townsville and Darwin, respectively. NWA possessed four RAAF medium bomb squadrons and two fighter squadrons, one RAF fighter squadron, one Dutch medium bomb squadron, and one USAAF heavy bomb squadron, later expanded to a four-squadron group. NEA's contribution to the campaign was limited to two squadrons of fighters.

The USAAF situation as the second phase of the campaign began was somewhat stagnant. The 5th Air Force had fewer numbers of both bombers and fighters by May 1943 than it had had about six months earlier, and only about half of these aircraft were operational. The Boeing B-17E/F equipped the 63rd, 64th, and 65th Squadrons, and the Consolidated B-24D heavy bombers equipped the 90th Bomb Group and the 403rd Squadron of the 43rd Bomb Group. In May 1943, the 380th Bomb Group's B-24Ds joined operations, flying initially from both New Guinea and NWA. North American B-25C/D medium bombers equipped the 3rd Bomb Group's 8th, 13th, and 90th Bomb Squadrons and the 38th Bomb Group's 71st and 405th Squadrons. The 22nd Bomb Group's 19th Bomb Squadron was the only unit flying Martin B-26 medium bombers, known as the "Silver Fleet" for their natural metal finish. The 3rd Bomb Group's 89th Bomb Squadron flew the Douglas A-20G light bomber.

During the campaign at least 70 percent of the B-25s of the USAAF and of RAAF No 18 Group were converted from level bombers to, or delivered as, "commerce destroyers" with various installations of additional forward-firing .50-caliber machine guns. Later, B-25Gs also had an M4 75mm cannon firing from the port side of the nose. This weapon was not popular with either air or ground personnel and its effectiveness against any but the smallest Japanese transports was not considered satisfactory. Its presence also meant those B-25s carried fewer .50-caliber machine guns, unacceptably reducing the forward firepower Kenney and others deemed necessary to silence antiaircraft guns at airfields or carried by ships. These aircraft were often retrofitted with .50-caliber nose guns in place of the cannon.

Regarding fighters, the Curtiss P-40 and Bell P-39 variants were still in use. Though suited for ground attack, progressive minor upgrades to the P-39 during the campaign did not remedy its basic air-to-air combat weaknesses. Its range was adequate for most base defense and escort duties and, like the P-40, it could extend its range using a belly drop tank. The 35th Fighter Group's 40th and 41st Squadrons upgraded to the P-39N and P-39Q in mid-1943, but P-39 variants were only flown by reconnaissance units in 1944. The P-40N became the standard variant, replacing the P-40E/Ks by mid-1943, though by mid-1944 only the 7th and 8th Fighter Squadrons flew the P-40N.

Some 823rd Bomb Squadron personnel watch a C-47 land at Wakde. Their B-25G pictured was factory-built with only two .50-caliber machine guns and a World War I-vintage, manually loaded M4 75mm cannon in its nose. This particular B-25 version was quite unpopular with both flight and maintenance personnel, due to cannon recoil airframe stress, aiming requirements, and reduced forward firepower. (MacArthur Memorial)

The Republic P-47D entered the campaign with the arrival of the 348th Fighter Group in June 1943. It was also used by the entire 58th Fighter Group and squadrons of the 8th, 35th, and 49th Fighter Groups at various times. Though it possessed ruggedness and firepower, and in combat could outdive any Japanese fighter, it was too short-legged for campaign operations without the use of external fuel tanks. These included the 200gal "Brisbane" belly tank, developed on Kenney's orders in Australia. Later, P-47D-15 models arrived with wing pylons capable of carrying two 165gal tanks like those used by the P-38. During the campaign, 5th Air Force flew the Lockheed P-38F, G, H, and J variants as they became available. Though much larger and heavier than its Japanese opponents, the P-38 had adequate maneuverability and excellent high-altitude performance. The P-38J, introduced in February 1944, possessed increased internal fuel capacity due to additional 55gal tanks in each wing leading edge. The 5th Air Force received kits and retrofitted older P-38 variants with this additional fuel tankage. Also on strength were the F-4/5 photo reconnaissance versions of the latest P-38 variants, assigned to the 8th, 25th, and 26th Photo Reconnaissance Squadrons.

There were enough Lockheed C-47/C-47A aircraft available throughout the campaign to meet Allied needs, though various RAAF aircraft were also employed in transport roles. Some converted B-17s were also used for transport. The C-47 was employed for cargo and personnel transport as well as paratroop/resupply drops.

The P-38 was the most important 5th Air Force fighter, possessing the range, firepower, and performance to escort bombers and effectively engage Japanese fighters. The light oval on the port engine of this 431st Fighter Squadron aircraft is a polished natural metal area the pilot used as a mirror to check that his landing gear was down. (NARA)

Several additional aircraft types or variants were used for maritime strike, reconnaissance, night fighting, transport, and air-sea rescue. The 17th Reconnaissance Squadron used B-25Ds with additional forward firepower, but they were not fully configured as strafers. Its sister 71st Reconnaissance Group unit, the 25th Liaison Squadron, mainly flew the Stinson L-5 Sentinel (piloted mostly by enlisted personnel) on reconnaissance, artillery spotting, clandestine insertion, downed aircrew rescue, and light personnel and cargo transport. The 20th Combat Mapping Squadron's F-7As, modified B-24s, carried six trimetrogon 2 × 18in cameras, three each in the nose and rear bomb bay, providing horizon-to-horizon photographic coverage. In October 1943, the 63rd Bomb Squadron began using XB-24 "Snoopers" (also called the SB-24). Modified for low-altitude night maritime strike, they carried the Low Altitude Bombardment equipment suite that included the SCR-717B radar, SCR-729 IFF interrogator, AN/APQ-5 low-altitude precision bombing attachment ("black box" computer), RC-217 auxiliary sighting unit, and the AN/ARN-1 radio altimeter. Additionally, other B-24 squadrons had a few aircraft fitted with air-sea-vessel (ASV) radar to aid location of Japanese ships or with special antennas and radio receivers to passively detect and locate Japanese radar equipment ("ferrets"). For reconnaissance, air-sea rescue, night bombing, and maritime strikes, SWPA's Fleet Air Wing 17 (FAW-17) had various US Navy (USN) patrol squadrons (VP) attached, equipped with Consolidated PBY-5A Catalinas that operated in conjunction with seaplane tenders at various locations around New Guinea. Finally, SWPA had a few night fighter units assigned, though they were mostly ineffective due to lack of proper equipment and training. They initially flew the Douglas P-70, an A-20 fitted with radar equipment, the B-25C, and the P-38. The more capable Northrop P-61 night fighter arrived in SWPA in June 1944.

The RAAF employed the Kittyhawk as its primary fighter throughout the campaign. It also operated four Supermarine Spitfire Vb squadrons, three in NWA (Nos 54 (RAF), 452, and 457) and one, No 79, assigned to No 73 Wing, first with No 9 Operational Group at Kiriwina and later with No 10 Operational Group at Momote and other airfields farther west.

For ground attack/support missions the RAAF possessed the Commonwealth Aircraft Corporation (CAC) Wirraway, CAC Boomerang, Bristol Beaufighter, Douglas Boston, and Vultee Vengeance. The Boomerang was designed and built in Australia to provide a single-seat alternative to the Wirraway. It performed the vital role of close air support to Allied ground forces, via both direct attacks and as a guide to other aircraft unfamiliar

The 58th Fighter Group, the last fighter unit to join 5th Air Force during the campaign, became operational from Dobodura on February 1, 1944. The group initially flew transport escort and airfield defense missions, but later transitioned into offensive escort and ground support. This 69th Fighter Squadron P-47D-15's underwing pylons allowed it to carry two 165gal drop tanks. (Claringbould)

with the trackless jungle where most battles were fought. The Wirraway was an Australian modification of the North American NA-16 trainer and performed as a light attack aircraft. The Beaufighter was a superb British attack aircraft that could also duel with Japanese bomber and reconnaissance aircraft under the right circumstances. The Boston and Vengeance were American designed and built, the former an A-20 that the RAAF modified as a bomber/strafer just like the 5th Air Force aircraft. The Vengeance, designed as a pure dive bomber, equipped four RAAF squadrons (Nos 12, 21, 23, and 24) during the campaign and performed adequately, although it was removed from New Guinea due to deficiencies in range, defensive armament, and bomb load. The Dutch No 18 Squadron, and later RAAF No 2 Squadron, operated B-25C/Ds from NWA, which were modified as bomber/strafers.

For bombing, torpedo strikes, and reconnaissance the RAAF flew the Bristol Beaufort. These operated from Milne Bay and Goodenough Island initially, supporting Solomon Sea and New Britain operations, and later moved west to deal with the IJA 18th Army. Nos 6 and 100 Squadrons performed conventional bombing while No 8 Squadron early on conducted maritime torpedo strike missions, but with indifferent results. In NWA, Nos 2 and 13 Squadrons flew Lockheed Hudsons on maritime attack and reconnaissance missions; No 2 later flew both Beauforts and B-25s. Also employed on a variety of missions was the Consolidated Catalina, with which the RAAF equipped Nos 11, 20, and 43 Squadrons. With a long range and heavy bomb load, the Catalina was able to reach any target in the theater, but its relatively slow speed made it vulnerable to antiaircraft fire and Japanese fighters in daylight. The RAAF Catalinas performed bombing, mining, maritime strike, reconnaissance, clandestine infiltration, and air-sea rescue missions; the RAAF also operated Black Cat variants. Additionally, the RAAF flew the Lockheed Lightning reconnaissance variant and a variety of light transport aircraft.

During the campaign Allied air power grew in lethality. In addition to successive upgraded variants of the American aircraft and the addition to the RAAF arsenal of the B-24 as the campaign came to a close, there were field modifications to improve capabilities. Nose turrets for the B-24Ds were initially installed in theater or in Hawaii. The 75mm cannon-armed B-25G was first a local modification to test its feasibility. A 1944 attempt to increase the A-20G's firepower by adding rockets failed, but it presaged later rocket arming of several types including the P-38 and Beaufighter.

No 4 Squadron Boomerangs flew ground support missions from Dobodura from July 1943. They later moved to Nadzab as part of No 10 Operational Group to support ground forces in the Huon Peninsula and later operations. This Boomerang sits at Nadzab near a 501st Bomb Squadron B-25 after completing a strafing mission near Saidor in February 1944. (AWM)

In June 1944, some A-20s were experimentally fitted with M8 4.5in (114mm) rockets in four three-rocket M10 launcher clusters [tubes loaded, inset]. However, they unacceptably limited aircraft aerodynamic performance and range. Of note, this 90th Bomb Squadron A-20G is an early production model originally intended for Lend-Lease to the USSR, evidenced by the 20mm cannons in its nose instead of .50-caliber machine guns. (NARA)

Airfields and air defense

The Allies began with seven airfields ("'dromes" in Australian parlance) within 30 miles of Port Moresby, a two-airstrip 'drome at Milne Bay and an expanding airstrip complex at Dobodura, north of the Owen Stanley Range. The relatively primitive condition of these and other airfields persisted throughout the campaign. Airbases in Australia, especially NWA, were only slightly better appointed. Some Japanese targets were beyond the reach of most Allied combat aircraft until additional forward airfields could be captured or developed. Bombers and fighters therefore often pre-staged to airstrips closer to their targets to top off fuel prior to flying missions. Airfields developed on New Guinea, New Britain, and the Admiralties during the campaign were in most cases simply areas cleared out of the jungle with runways and taxiways alternately turning into quagmires or dusty tracks until proper surfacing and drainage were completed. Even with the use of asphalt, crushed coral, and American perforated steel plank (PSP, or Marston mats) on runways to provide stability and traction, operations at these airfields were often quite difficult. In some locations the soil was adequate for transport, fighter, and medium bomber operations, but it was not capable of supporting heavy bomber operations. Proper living and messing quarters, administrative buildings, maintenance shelters, dispersal hardstands, and protective revetments had to be built over time. Personnel often lived and worked in tents or crude shelters made from scrounged lumber and jungle growth and dove into waterlogged slit trenches to avoid air attack.

Responsibility for all facets of air defense fell under ADVON, but air warning and antiaircraft defense of the New Guinea airfields was problematic. As the Allied build-up progressed, there were numerous Australian and American radar sites established along with ground spotters. But their data was provided haphazardly to units with overlapping responsibilities in radar warning, fighter direction, and antiaircraft defense. Thus, the US 565th and 583rd Air Warning Battalions and the various fighter groups' fighter control squadrons sometimes passed conflicting orders to fighters. This situation was not resolved until mid-1944 with the stand-up of the US 85th Air Defense Wing and the institution of processes to compile radar and observational data at filter centers, where the fighter control squadron personnel would direct Allied fighters to intercept Japanese aircraft. Antiaircraft defenses were similarly confused until the 14th Antiaircraft Command was activated on November 15, 1943. As each new air facility was established during the campaign, Browning .50-caliber machine guns were immediately set up in an antiaircraft role until heavier guns were emplaced. These heavier weapons were various 20mm, 40mm, and 90mm guns.

DEFENDER'S CAPABILITIES

A Lily of the 75th Air Regiment, one of four air regiments equipped with Lilys during the campaign. The 45th and 208th Air Regiments' Lilys carried out the lion's share of IJAAF bombing efforts in New Guinea. The aircraft was disliked by its crews for its light bomb load, poor flight characteristics, and weak defensive armament. (AC)

The Japanese realized control of the air was critical in New Guinea and tried to deploy sufficient air force to the region to achieve victory. As part of the Army–Navy Central Agreement on Southeast Area Operations of March 1943, New Guinea was the focal point of Japanese air operations and the IJA and IJN agreed to build up their air strength in the region. The IJA Air Force's (IJAAF) goal was to have 240 aircraft of all types by September 1943 and the IJN Air Force (IJNAF) agreed to bring its strength up to 357 aircraft by the end of June. The IJNAF total was exclusive of any carrier aircraft that could be temporarily moved from their parent ships at Truk Atoll down to Rabaul. Up to April 1944, the IJAAF moved 1,800 aircraft and 2,000 pilots to the region. Both the IJAAF and IJNAF moved most of their newly manufactured aircraft to the New Guinea and Solomons fronts until March 1944.

The IJAAF

The IJAAF role in the New Guinea air campaign was performed mainly by 4th Air Army, under the command of Lt Gen. Teramoto Kumaichi. Originally an infantry officer, Teramoto switched to the Imperial Army's air arm in 1933 where he spent the rest of his career. In May 1943, he assumed command of 1st Air Army based in Japan. When 4th Air Army was formed to direct air operations in New Guinea, Teramoto was given command in July 1943. Following defeat in New Guinea, he resumed his career on the IJAAF's staff and later in 1945 assumed command of the entire IJAAF. He committed ritual suicide after Japan's surrender.

The initial IJAAF unit responsible for New Guinea operations was 6th Air Division. This formation was under the command of Lt Gen. Itabana Giichi. His tenure witnessed a series of disasters and he was relieved after the series of attacks against the Japanese airbases at Hollandia in 1944.

As the weight of Allied air operations in New Guinea increased, in mid-1943 IGHQ transferred 7th Air Division from Ambon in the NEI to the New Guinea front. To command the larger force, 4th Air Army Headquarters was established. The first 7th Air Division elements arrived at Wewak on July 25 and immediately began operations. In early November, 7th Air Division was ordered to return to Ambon to prepare for operations to defend the newly designated national defense line. The 7th Air Division was brought under the command of 2nd Area Army for the defense of western New Guinea. It was still headquartered on Ambon where it was trying to rebuild after heavy losses between August and November 1943. In early 1944, it possessed an operational strength of about 50 aircraft and was devoted almost exclusively to escorting convoys in the rear areas.

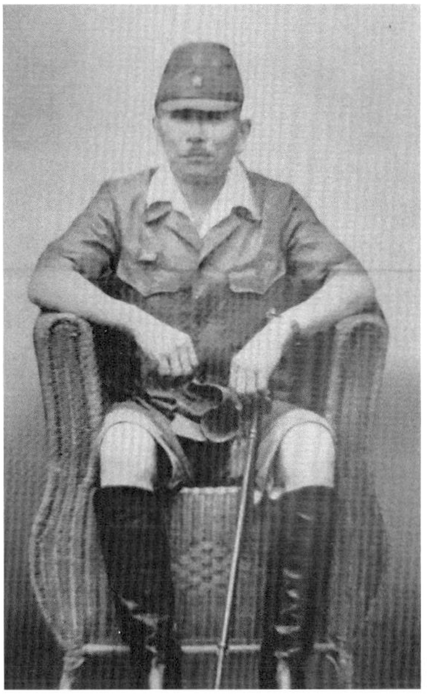

Teramoto Kumaichi commanded 4th Air Army in New Guinea from August 1943. During his tenure, Teramoto had first call on IJAAF resources. Despite this, he was unable to halt or even seriously delay the Allied advance in New Guinea. He shifted his headquarters to the Celebes in April 1944. (AC)

IJAAF aircraft

The basic IJAAF unit was the air regiment. It had a nominal strength of 45 aircraft, but in New Guinea the air regiments were never brought up to full strength. Each had more pilots or crews than aircraft, and the more experienced flyers got the majority of flight time. Accordingly, they were exposed to greater losses, while less experienced pilots received fewer opportunities to learn the skills necessary to survive in combat. Aircraft serviceability was also low due to lack of spare parts, and ground and air crews were incapacitated by combat losses or tropical diseases. When Wewak and Hollandia were surrounded by the Allies in 1944, most IJAAF ground crews were not evacuated; but fought as infantry or conducted long retreats. The same fate awaited even some of the aviators.

The most numerous IJAAF fighter in New Guinea was the Nakajima Ki-43 Army Type 1 Fighter. Often confused with the similar looking IJNAF Mitsubishi A6M Zero fighter by Allied pilots, it received the Allied reporting name of Oscar. It was flown at various times by every IJAAF fighter unit serving in New Guinea, sometimes as a replacement for other fighter types lost by those units. Principal units flying the Oscar were the 1st, 11th, 24th, 33rd, 59th, 63rd, 77th, and 248th Air Regiments. Though possessing good range and great maneuverability, the Oscar was a mediocre aircraft compared with more modern Allied fighters in both speed and armament. Against the P-38 and the P-47, the Oscar was badly outclassed.

Despite its great promise, the Kawasaki Ki-61 Army Type 3 Fighter failed to meet expectations. In the early months of 1943, the situation in New Guinea demanded that

A Tony on Formosa awaiting transfer to the New Guinea theater. The Tony was Japan's only liquid-cooled, in-line engined fighter. Its Ha-40 engine was a maintenance nightmare and the type had a relatively low operational rate. Tonys equipped the 68th and 78th Air Regiments during the campaign. (AC)

the Ki-61, known by its Allied reporting name of Tony, be rushed into service. It was flown by both the 68th and 78th Air Regiments. When the Tony performed as designed, it was the best IJAAF fighter in the South Pacific. Its speed could match that of the P-38 in level flight. Many of the variants used in New Guinea carried two wing-mounted 20mm Mauser cannon in place of 12.7mm machine guns. However, its external auxiliary fuel tanks made the aircraft tail heavy, causing it to pitch up. This resulted in stalls during takeoffs and landings and the deaths of many pilots.

Many other technical problems limited the effectiveness of the Tony. Its Ha-40 engine, a license-produced German Daimler-Benz DB 601A, was the source of many problems. In particular, its Mitsubishi fuel injection system proved troublesome compared with the original German Bosch system, for which the Japanese failed to procure a license to produce. The fuel injection pump issue caused the engine to stop abruptly. There was also an issue with the propellor pitch control. When this occurred, the aircraft could not climb properly. Mechanics in New Guinea were not trained to work on the Tony. Making things worse, no spare parts were available. Major overhaul of the Ha-40 was virtually impossible in the conditions prevailing on New Guinea, and the nearest repair facility was on Halmahera Island, some 930 miles from Wewak. Many of the Tonys delivered to New Guinea were unfit for duty because of uncorrected production defects.

The final type of IJAAF fighter seen in the skies over New Guinea was the Kawasaki Ki-45 Army Type 2 two-seat fighter, later given the reporting name Nick by the Allies. The Nick was used by the 5th and 13th Air Regiments. It was comparatively fast and carried heavy armament. The Nick was not maneuverable enough to contend with Allied fighters, but it did have success against unescorted bombers. A night fighter version with oblique-firing 20mm guns was also developed. The Nick also proved successful against Allied shipping with its heavy nose armament.

Throughout the New Guinea campaign, the IJAAF was handicapped by its lack of offensive power; its bombers were few in number and possessed inferior technical capabilities. The standard IJAAF light bomber of the period was the Kawasaki Ki-48 Army Type 99 twin-engine light bomber (given the reporting name Lily). The Lily was used by the 34th, 45th, 75th, and 208th Air Regiments. It was thoroughly inferior in all respects to its Allied counterparts. The Lily lacked the speed to escape from enemy fighters, lacked armor protection for its crew and fuel tanks, possessed weak defensive armament of only three machine guns, and carried a small payload.

In addition to light bomber units, the IJAAF possessed significant numbers of aircraft that it classified as heavy bombers. In reality, these were twin-engine aircraft with smaller payload capabilities than Allied medium bombers. The first modern IJAAF "heavy" bomber was the Mitsubishi Ki-21 Army Type 97 Heavy Bomber, later given the Allied reporting name of Sally. Possessing relatively slow speed, light payload, and weak defensive armament, the Sally was obsolescent in the face of Allied fighter opposition. Two units, the 14th and 60th Air Regiments, operated the Sally in the region.

Unfortunately for the IJAAF, the replacement for the Sally offered little additional capability. The Nakajima Ki-49 Army Type 100 Heavy Bomber Helen was flown by the 7th and 61st Air Regiments. Speed was comparable to the Sally, as was the bomb load. The Helen possessed better protection and good defensive armament, but its engines were unreliable. Crews preferred the Sally because of its ease of maintenance and flying. The Helen was never available in large numbers and missions were seldom flown with more than six aircraft. On the majority of missions against land targets, 110lb bombs were carried. Against maritime targets, 220lb bombs were used. The majority of Helen missions were not offensive – convoy escort missions were the most common type of sortie. In December 1943, after heavy losses attempting to counter the Allied landing on Cape Gloucester on New Britain, 6th Air Division ordered that the Helen no longer be committed on daylight offensive operations, and by April 1944 the type had been withdrawn to the NEI.

A small number of Mitsubishi Ki-51 Type 99 Reconnaissance/Assault Planes were also used by the IJAAF during the campaign. It was well liked because it was easy to fly and maintain. Given the Allied reporting name Sonia, the Ki-51a was the reconnaissance version, first operating from Lae in May 1943 with the 83rd Independent Squadron. The K-51b version was a light attack bomber with a 441lb payload and three machine guns.

Probably the most successful IJAAF aircraft of the campaign was the Mitsubishi Ki-46 Army Type 100 Command Reconnaissance Plane Dinah. Due to its impressive performance, the Dinah operated early on with virtual impunity in Allied airspace. Later versions of the P-38 could intercept the Dinah and losses began to mount, but it remained elusive at high altitudes. The type operated in the theater throughout the campaign.

The 4th Air Army used the Sonia for reconnaissance and ground attack. In the former role it equipped the 70th and 83rd Independent Squadrons and 6th Air Division Headquarters. In the latter role it equipped the 26th Air Regiment, one Sonia of which is shown here abandoned at But. (AWM)

The IJNAF

The 11th Air Fleet, headquartered at Rabaul, was responsible for overseeing IJNAF operations in New Guinea. Vice Admiral (V. Adm.) Kusaka Jinichi assumed command of 11th Air Fleet on October 8, 1942, and of the Southeast Area Fleet in December 1942. Kusaka was not a naval aviator and had little background in aviation; in the IJN it was not unusual for non-aviators to command aviation formations. However, he was considered an aggressive commander. During 1943, the 11th generally focused on the defense of Rabaul. Exceptions were made to react to some Allied landings on New Guinea's Huon Peninsula and on New Britain. The Allies' IJNAF antagonist in western New Guinea in 1943–44, which was inside Japan's inner defense zone, was the 23rd Air Flotilla based at Kendari in the Celebes. By early 1944, it was down to an operational strength of about 50 aircraft and most of its experienced pilots had been transferred to Rabaul over the course of 1943.

IJNAF operations over New Guinea relied almost exclusively on two types of aircraft. The principal strike aircraft was the Mitsubishi G4M1 Navy Type 1 Attack Bomber, later given the reporting name Betty. Against Allied defenses Betty units suffered heavy losses and were eventually restricted to night attacks. The Betty's impressive range was gained at the expense of armor protection and self-sealing fuel tanks, so that when hit the Betty tended to burst into flames. Another issue was its modest payload and mediocre defensive armament, though it possessed a tail-mounted 20mm cannon.

The most numerically important IJNAF aircraft during this period was the Mitsubishi A6M2/3/5 Model 21/22/32/52 Type 0 Carrier Fighter. It was given the Allied reporting names of Zeke, Hap, and Hamp, based on the model, but it was almost universally referred to as the Zero. Against inferior Allied aircraft the Zero possessed superior range, speed, and maneuverability, and also possessed superior climbing capabilities and good acceleration compared to most Allied fighters. But the Zero's lack of adequate protective armor and self-sealing fuel tanks made it vulnerable to battle damage. Of lesser importance was the IJNAF's standard dive bomber, the Aichi D3A2 Navy Type 99 Carrier Bomber (Allied reporting name Val). Though a capable dive bomber, it was handicapped by a small payload and vulnerability to interception.

V. Adm. Kusaka Jinichi, headquartered at Rabaul, commanded all IJNAF units assigned to the South Pacific. Although the IJNAF participated in the New Guinea campaign in 1943, due to an IJA–IJN agreement Kusaka's attention and force allocation were mainly directed toward the Solomons, leaving the IJAAF to contend with 5th Air Force on New Guinea. (AC)

The Mitsubishi A6M2/3/5 Zero was the premier IJNAF fighter. Several units, known unofficially as the 'Rabaul Air Group', operated from Rabaul during the campaign equipped with this aircraft. This 204 Air Group Zero, an early Model 52, scrambles to defend Rabaul, as shown by its lack of a long-range drop tank. (AC)

Early warning and antiaircraft protection

The IJA possessed radar, most based on American and British equipment captured earlier in the war. However, these sets were unreliable and were inferior in terms of performance compared with Allied radar. There were radars at Rabaul and Wewak, and Manokwari in western New Guinea, but it is not known whether other airfields were equipped with radar. In any event, though raid information was at least occasionally passed by radio between the IJNAF and IJAAF, there was no comprehensive warning system to quickly handle whatever information became available. The Japanese also made use of ground- or ship-based spotters like the Allies, but these could at best provide warning only a short time before an attack. Factors in favor of the Japanese were terrain and weather. Using these, the Japanese could often predict the timing and even the direction to be used by attacking Allied aircraft.

Early in the campaign, Japanese antiaircraft fire was inaccurate and ineffective. The Imperial Army's standard antiaircraft weapons were principally responsible for this failure. For protection against medium-altitude attack, the obsolescent Type 88 75mm antiaircraft gun was often employed. Its replacement, the Type 4, was not introduced until 1944, and only 70 were produced. The Type 88 was not able to adjust rapidly to a target's changing altitude, speed, and direction. The most common light antiaircraft weapon of the Imperial Army was the Type 98 20mm machine cannon. It was respected for its robust design and mobility, but it possessed mediocre performance characteristics and relied on 20-round magazines, which reduced its effective rate of fire. The Japanese also tended to place antiaircraft weapons close to the area to be defended, often within a mile of a runway. This did increase the volume of fire over the Allied target, but it reduced the length of time that the guns could engage aircraft at low altitudes. In November 1943, the Japanese changed to a dispersal deployment pattern that increased the time attacking aircraft were under fire.

Antiaircraft fire was the major threat to Allied aircraft during airfield attacks, so these sites were always prime targets. At this Boram antiaircraft position shown on November 27, 1943, at least five Type 88 75mm cannon are ready for action. (NARA/AWM)

CAMPAIGN OBJECTIVES

Attacker's objectives

MacArthur's ultimate desire to retake the Philippines never wavered, and he was in competition with the adjacent Pacific Ocean Area (POA) theater commanded by Adm. Chester Nimitz, since the two principal commanders in the Pacific had different visions on the best strategy to defeat Japan. However, both agreed that the Japanese base at Rabaul had to be destroyed prior to any push westward.

Seizing or building airfields was the Allies' chief campaign objective. The V Fighter Commander, Brig. Gen. Wurtsmith (center, back to camera), and a staff officer flew P-38s into Tadji on April 24, 1944, to inspect its future operational potential. Meanwhile, RAAF No 62 Works Wing quickly readies Tadji for general use. (AWM)

The US–UK Casablanca Conference in January 1943 set general, if somewhat ambitious, guidelines for Pacific operations for that year. The follow-on March Pacific Military Conference in Washington, during which MacArthur's representatives, including Kenney, argued strongly for a strategy focused on reaching Japan through New Guinea and the Philippines, modified the goals for 1943 based on a more realistic appraisal of the forces available. The result was a compromise between SWPA and POA that would have both theaters attacking westward along parallel axes. The JCS's directive issued on March 28, 1943, gave SWPA the tasks of establishing airfields on Kiriwina Island, seizing key locations on the northeast New Guinea coast – Lae, Finschhafen, and Madang – and seizing western New Britain. MacArthur was allowed to exercise strategic direction over Adm. Halsey's SOPAC theater, which was tasked with operating an airfield on Woodlark Island and occupying the Solomons up to southern Bougainville. All these operations (and future ones) had as their main objective seizing or developing airfields to support further Allied moves westward and were to proceed as the Japanese resistance allowed, rather than in a rigidly prescribed order.

Once the overall direction for the campaign was set, MacArthur developed the *Elkton III* plan, in consultation with Halsey, to cover all subordinate tasks. Each operation was to be timed for mutual support between the SWPA and SOPAC theaters, with the schedule left in terms of weeks or months between operations. Joint communications links and cooperative reconnaissance plans were also arranged. MacArthur's General Headquarters (GHQ) staff issued the plan on April 26. Those operations directed at encircling Rabaul fell under *Cartwheel*. For SWPA these were the seizure of Kiriwina and Woodlark Islands (Operation *I*); seizure of Lae (Operation *IIa*),

CAMPAIGN THEATER EAST AND WEST: MAY 1943 AND FEBRUARY 1944

Balikpapan
Menado
Galela
Miti
Lolobata
Ternate
HALMAHERA
Jefman
Mar
Middleburg
Sansapor
Samate
Sorong
Manokwari
VOGELKOP PENINSULA
Mumi
NOEMFOOR ISLAND
BIAK
OWI
CELEBES
Namlea
BOEROE ISLAND
CERAM
Ambon
Kokas
Fakfak
Babo
Utarom
Kaimana
Geelvink Bay
Nabire
MacCluer Gulf
Kendari
Makassar
Banda Sea
Langgoer
KAI ISLAND
Dobo
ARU ISLAND
Taberfane
Flores Sea
TANIMBAR ISLAND
Saumlaki
SELARU ISLAND
Cape Chater
Lautem
Dili
TIMOR
Koepang
Penfui
Sarmi
Wakde
Arare
Hollandia
Aitape
Tadji
But
Dagua
Wewak
Boram
Hansa Bay
NEW GUINEA
Lorengau
Momote
ADMIRALTY ISLANDS
EMIRAU ISLAND
NEW HANOVER
Kavieng
Panapai
NEW IRELAND
BISMARCK ARCHIPELAGO
Rabaul
GREEN ISLAND
Vitiaz Strait
Dampier Strait
C. Gloucester
Borgen Bay
Talasea
C. Hoskins
NEW BRITAIN
Arawe
Gasmata
Lindenhafen
Alexishafen
Madang
Bogadjim
Saidor
Gusap
Dumpu
Sio
Finschhafen
Nadzab
Tsili Tsili
Lae
Hopoi
Marilinan
Wau
Huon Gulf
Salamaua
Solomon Sea
GOODENOUGH ISLAND
Kiriwina
KIRIWINA ISLAND
Buna
Dobodura
Oro Bay
Vivigani
WOODLARK ISLAND
Port Moresby
Turnbull
Gurney
Milne Bay
SAMARAI
NIMOA
C. Kombies
Merauke
Torres Strait
Arafura Sea
Horn Island
BATHURST ISLAND
Darwin
C. Fourcroy
Winnellie
Strauss
Hughes
Livingston
Coomalie Creek
McDonald
Long
Manbulloo
Fenton
Gould
Batchelor
Millingimbi
Timor Sea
Coral Sea
Cairns
Mareeba
Karumba
AUSTRALIA
WESTERN AUSTRALIA
NORTHERN TERRITORY
Townsville
Corunna Downs
N
0
200 miles
0
200km

ALLIED ORDER OF BATTLE

May 1943

NO 9 OPERATIONAL GROUP; NORTH-WESTERN/NORTH-EASTERN AREAS

Unit	Aircraft	Base
No 1 Rescue & Communications Squadron	Various	Port Moresby
No 2 Squadron	Hudson	Hughes
No 4 Squadron	Wirraway	Port Moresby
No 6 Squadron	Hudson	Milne Bay
No 7 Squadron	Beaufort	Horn Island
No 11 Squadron	Catalina	Cairns
No 12 Squadron	Vengeance	Batchelor
No 13 Squadron	Hudson	Hughes
No 18 Squadron (Dutch)	B-25	McDonald
No 20 Squadron	Catalina	Cairns
No 22 Squadron	Boston	Port Moresby
No 30 Squadron	Beaufighter	Port Moresby
No 31 Squadron	Beaufighter	Coomalie Creek
No 43 Squadron	Catalina	Cairns
No 54 Squadron (RAF)	Spitfire	Winnellie
No 75 Squadron	Kittyhawk	Milne Bay
No 77 Squadron	Kittyhawk	Milne Bay
No 84 Squadron	Boomerang	Horn Island
No 100 Squadron	Beaufort	Milne Bay
No 452 Squadron	Spitfire	Strauss
No 457 Squadron	Spitfire	Livingston

USAAF 5TH AIR FORCE

Unit	Aircraft	Base
3rd Bomb Group (M)		
8th Bomb Squadron	B-25	Dobodura
13th Bomb Squadron	B-25	Dobodura
89th Bomb Squadron	A-20	Dobodura
90th Bomb Squadron	B-25	Dobodura
38th Bomb Group (M)		
71st Bomb Squadron	B-25	Port Moresby
405th Bomb Squadron	B-25	Port Moresby
43rd Bomb Group (H)		
63rd Bomb Squadron	B-17	Port Moresby
64th Bomb Squadron	B-17	Port Moresby
65th Bomb Squadron	B-17	Port Moresby
403rd Bomb Squadron	B-17/B-24	Mareeba
90th Bomb Group (H)		
319th Bomb Squadron	B-24	Fenton
320th Bomb Squadron	B-24	Port Moresby
321st Bomb Squadron	B-24	Port Moresby
400th Bomb Squadron	B-24	Port Moresby
380th Bomb Group (H)		
528th Bomb Squadron	B-24	Fenton
529th Bomb Squadron	B-24	Manbulloo
530th Bomb Squadron	B-24	Fenton
531st Bomb Squadron	B-24	Manbulloo
8th Fighter Group		
35th Fighter Squadron	P-39	Port Moresby
36th Fighter Squadron	P-39/P-400	Port Moresby
80th Fighter Squadron	P-38	Port Moresby
35th Fighter Group		
39th Fighter Squadron	P-38	Port Moresby
40th Fighter Squadron	P-39	Port Moresby
41st Fighter Squadron	P-39	Port Moresby
49th Fighter Group		
7th Fighter Squadron	P-40	Dobodura
8th Fighter Squadron	P-40	Dobodura
9th Fighter Squadron	P-38	Dobodura
317th Troop Carrier Group (partial)	C-47	Port Moresby
374th Troop Carrier Group	C-47	Port Moresby
6th Night Fighter Squadron (det)	P-70	Port Moresby
8th Photo Reconnaissance Squadron	F-5	Port Moresby

ALLIED ORDER OF BATTLE

February 1944

NO 9, 10 OPERATIONAL GROUPS; NORTH-WESTERN/NORTH-EASTERN AREAS

Unit	Aircraft	Base
No 2 Squadron	Hudson	Hughes
No 4 Squadron	Wirraway	Port Moresby
No 6 Squadron	Beaufort	Vivigani
No 7 Squadron	Beaufort	Horn Island
No 8 Squadron	Beaufort	Vivigani
No 11 Squadron	Catalina	Cairns
No 12 Squadron	Vengeance	Batchelor
No 13 Squadron	Hudson	Hughes
No 18 Squadron (Dutch)	B-25	McDonald
No 20 Squadron	Catalina	Cairns
No 21 Squadron	Vengeance	Nadzab
No 22 Squadron	Boston	Kiriwina
No 23 Squadron	Vengeance	Nadzab
No 24 Squadron	Vengeance	Nadzab
No 30 Squadron	Beaufighter	Kiriwina
No 31 Squadron	Beaufighter	Coomalie Creek
No 100 Squadron	Beaufort	Milne Bay
No 43 Squadron	Catalina	Karumba
No 54 Squadron (RAF)	Spitfire	Winnellie
No 75 Squadron	Kittyhawk	Nadzab
No 76 Squadron	Kittyhawk	Kiriwina
No 77 Squadron	Kittyhawk	Milne Bay
No 78 Squadron	Kittyhawk	Nadzab
No 79 Squadron	Spitfire	Kiriwina
No 84 Squadron	Kittyhawk	Horn Island
No 86 Squadron	Kittyhawk	Merauke
No 100 Squadron	Beaufort	Vivigani
No 452 Squadron	Spitfire	Strauss
No 457 Squadron	Spitfire	Livingstone

USAAF 5TH AIR FORCE

Unit	Aircraft	Base
3rd Bomb Group (M)		
8th Bomb Squadron	A-20	Nadzab
13th Bomb Squadron	A-20	Nadzab
89th Bomb Squadron	A-20	Nadzab
90th Bomb Squadron	A-20	Nadzab
22nd Bomb Group (H)		
2nd Bomb Squadron	B-24	Nadzab
19th Bomb Squadron	B-24	Nadzab
33rd Bomb Squadron	B-24	Nadzab
408th Bomb Squadron	B-24	Nadzab
38th Bomb Group (M)		
71st Bomb Squadron	B-25	Port Moresby
405th Bomb Squadron	B-25	Port Moresby
822nd Bomb Squadron	B-25	Port Moresby
823rd Bomb Squadron	B-25	Port Moresby
43rd Bomb Group (H)		
63rd Bomb Squadron	XB-24 (SB-24)	Nadzab
64th Bomb Squadron	B-24	Nadzab
65th Bomb Squadron	B-24	Nadzab
403rd Bomb Squadron	B-24	Nadzab
90th Bomb Group (H)		
319th Bomb Squadron	B-24	Nadzab
320th Bomb Squadron	B-24	Nadzab
321st Bomb Squadron	B-24	Nadzab
400th Bomb Squadron	B-24	Nadzab
312th Bomb Group (M)		
386th Bomb Squadron	A-20	Gusap
387th Bomb Squadron	A-20	Gusap
388th Bomb Squadron	A-20	Gusap
389th Bomb Squadron	A-20	Gusap
345th Bomb Group (M)		
498th Bomb Squadron	B-25	Nadzab
499th Bomb Squadron	B-25	Nadzab
500th Bomb Squadron	B-25	Nadzab
501st Bomb Squadron	B-25	Nadzab
380th Bomb Group (H)		
528th Bomb Squadron	B-24	Fenton
529th Bomb Squadron	B-24	Long
530th Bomb Squadron	B-24	Fenton
531st Bomb Squadron	B-24	Long
417th Bomb Group (M)		
672nd Bomb Squadron	A-20	Dobodura
673rd Bomb Squadron	A-20	Dobodura
674th Bomb Squadron	A-20	Dobodura
675th Bomb Squadron	A-20	Dobodura
8th Fighter Group		
35th Fighter Squadron	P-40	Cape Gloucester
36th Fighter Squadron	P-47	Finschhafen
80th Fighter Squadron	P-38	Cape Gloucester
35th Fighter Group		
39th Fighter Squadron	P-47	Gusap
40th Fighter Squadron	P-47	Gusap
41st Fighter Squadron	P-47	Gusap
49th Fighter Group		
7th Fighter Squadron	P-40	Gusap
8th Fighter Squadron	P-40	Gusap
9th Fighter Squadron	P-38/P-47	Gusap
58th Fighter Group		
69th Fighter Squadron	P-47	Dobodura
310th Fighter Squadron	P-47	Dobodura
311th Fighter Squadron	P-47	Dobodura
348th Fighter Group		
340th Fighter Squadron	P-47	Finschhafen
341st Fighter Squadron	P-47	Finschhafen
342nd Fighter Squadron	P-47	Finschhafen
475th Fighter Group		
431st Fighter Squadron	P-38	Dobodura
432nd Fighter Squadron	P-38	Dobodura
433rd Fighter Squadron	P-38	Dobodura
6th Photo Reconnaissance Group		
8th Photo Reconnaissance Squadron	F-5	Port Moresby
20th Photo Reconnaissance Squadron	F-7	Nadzab
25th Photo Reconnaissance Squadron	F-5	Nadzab
26th Photo Reconnaissance Squadron	F-5	Finschhafen
71st Reconnaissance Group		
17th Reconnaissance Squadron	B-25	Dobodura
25th Liaison Squadron	L-5	Nadzab
82nd Reconnaissance Squadron	P-39	Dobodura
110th Reconnaissance Squadron	P-39	Gusap

USN FLEET AIR WING-17

Unit	Aircraft	Base
VP-33	PBY-5A	Samarai
VP-34	PBY-5A	Samarai
VP-52	PBY-5A	Nimoa

Finschhafen (Operation *IIb*), and Madang (Operation *IIc*) on New Guinea; the taking of Cape Gloucester and Arawe (Operation *IIIa*); and the taking of Gasmata and neutralization of Talasea (Operation *IIIb*), all on New Britain. To execute these SWPA operations, MacArthur had the Allied Air Forces under Kenney, the Allied Land Forces under Australian Gen. Sir Thomas Blamey, and the Allied Naval Forces under USN V. Adm. Arthur Carpender. The ground force was divided between Blamey's New Guinea Force, generally responsible for combat on New Guinea, and Alamo Force, subordinate directly to GHQ and headed by US Army Lt Gen. Walter Krueger, initially responsible for combat on New Britain and other islands.

On June 30, the Allies executed Operation *Chronicle*, the unopposed amphibious landings on Kiriwina and Woodlark. Once Alamo Force took Kiriwina, RAAF engineers moved to establish airfields as quickly as possible. An airbase on Kiriwina, 270nm from Rabaul, would bring other SWPA aircraft besides heavy bombers within range of more New Britain targets. Also on June 30, to further Operation *IIa*, a battalion combat team of the US 162nd Infantry Regiment, the MacKechnie Force, landed at Nassau Bay to assist the Australian 17th Brigade battling elements of the IJA 51st Division around Salamaua.

The August 1943 Quadrant CCS conference had decided that isolation of Rabaul, rather than its capture, would suffice while Nimitz's POA forces pushed ahead in the Central Pacific theater. This removed the need for MacArthur to seize New Britain, but the rest of his tasks remained unchanged. The Allies thus made major advances in September to seize New Guinea's Markham River Valley and Huon Peninsula. Over September 4–5, the Allies implemented *Postern* (Operation *IIa/b*) when the VII Amphibious Force (VII Amphib) of the Allied Naval Forces landed the Australian 9th Division just east of Lae on September 4, and the next day 5th Air Force dropped the US 503rd Parachute Infantry Regiment and Australian engineers about 18 miles west of Lae at Nadzab. Thereafter, once a landing strip had been cleared the Australian 7th Division was flown into Nadzab and began pushing east to form a pincer against Lae with the 9th Division pushing west. Lae was captured on September 16. Next, on September 22, VII Amphib delivered the Australian 20th Brigade about five miles north of Finschhafen, which was seized on October 2. However, additional moves were needed for the Allies to secure control of the Vitiaz and Dampier Straits, which both sides considered vital to their regional strategic positions.

The next Allied moves came on New Britain in execution of *Dexterity* (Operation *IIIa*). This involved amphibious landings at Gasmata on December 15 and at Cape Gloucester on December 26. The former objective, which was changed to Arawe on November 21, served to distract the Japanese from the latter. The Cape Gloucester landing involved the US 1st

After the Allies seized Nadzab on September 5 they quickly readied it for air operations. C-47s flew the Australian 7th Division there to begin its move east to capture Lae. Here, 7th Division troops unload their material from 433rd Troop Carrier Group C-47s at Nadzab on September 11. (NARA)

Marine Division, the only time the Marines were involved in an SWPA landing. Both landings were lightly opposed and made steady progress toward securing western New Britain against Japanese counterattack and solidifying Allied control of the straits. The final move came on January 2, when VII Amphib put the 126th Regimental Combat Team of the US 32nd Infantry Division ashore at Saidor. This not only seized a valuable airfield near the straits, but also cut the coastal link between the IJA 20th Division at Sio and 18th Army Headquarters at Wewak. It also officially completed *Cartwheel*, although Rabaul was yet to be fully encircled.

The next phase of MacArthur's push westward, codified in his Reno III plan of October 1943 and approved by the CCS at the December Sextant conference, included an assault at Hansa Bay by April 26, about 100 miles west of Saidor. However, it appeared by early February that the Allies might be able to skip Hansa Bay and strike further west. It also appeared that the Allies could take the Admiralty Islands earlier than originally planned and with far less effort. These reassessments were based in large measure on ULTRA decrypts made possible by exploiting cipher material seized in January by Australian troops at Sio that was imperfectly buried by retreating 20th Division IJA troops. Since intelligence showed that fewer IJA troops were defending Hollandia than Madang, Hansa Bay, or Wewak, MacArthur revised his plans.

After aerial reconnaissance of the Admiralties disclosed no IJA activity on Los Negros Island, MacArthur authorized a "reconnaissance in force" that, though opposed, seized Momote airfield and provided the springboard for the capture of Los Negros and Manus Islands by March 9. Manus possessed both Lorengau airfield and the spacious Seeadler Harbor that could be used by Allied forces to push toward both the Palaus and the Philippines, and Mokerang airfield was built on Los Negros by April. The Admiralties' capture, along with SOPAC's seizure of Nissan (Green) Island on February 15 and Emirau Island on March 20, made the capture of Kavieng, like that of Rabaul, unnecessary.

These successes and apparent Japanese weakness led MacArthur to issue *Reno IV* to accelerate the capture of Hollandia (Operation *Reckless*) by six months, from October to April 1944. This was his most daring and effective stroke of the campaign. He decided to bypass Wewak and instead seize Hollandia, a weakly defended though important Japanese air and sea base. On April 22, 1944, VII Amphib, supported briefly by Nimitz's Fast Carrier Task Force, staged landings of the 24th and 41st Infantry Divisions at two points near Hollandia and at Aitape, 125 miles to the southeast, to capture the airfields at those locations. The Japanese were caught by surprise and out of position, and the captured airfields were operating by April 28, though they were never suitable for heavy bomber operations. The Allies then seized Wakde Island with its coral airstrip on May 18, using it as a fighter and medium bomber staging base to support their next major step. This was the seizure of Biak, an island in Geelvink Bay in northwestern New Guinea. It was attacked on May 27, but stiff IJA resistance kept its three airfields from full Allied operations until late June. Meanwhile, the small island of Owi, three miles southeast of Biak, and Noemfoor, about 75 miles west in Geelvink Bay, were occupied on June 8 and July 2, respectively. Both possessed airfields that the Allies put quickly into operation. These acquisitions allowed the final operation to move forward when on July 30 and 31 the Allies seized Mar and Sansapor, respectively, on New Guinea's westernmost coastal area, gaining two more airfields from which to launch MacArthur's long-awaited campaign to retake the Philippines.

Gen. Douglas MacArthur's conduct of the New Guinea campaign reflected his desire to reconquer the Philippines. He believed rapid progress in New Guinea was essential for the JCS to agree with this objective. His accelerated operation to capture Hollandia was especially ambitious. Here, he strides ashore with 24th Infantry Division troops at Hollandia on April 22, 1944. (NARA)

OPPOSITE SWPA OPERATIONS

MacArthur's campaign moved swiftly to isolate Rabaul and make progress toward retaking the Philippines.

Defenders' objectives

The Army–Navy Central Agreement on Southeast Area Operations issued by IGHQ on March 25, 1943, included a shift in emphasis to New Guinea from the Solomons. In particular, Lt Gen. Adachi Hatazo's 18th Army was to hold the Lae–Salamaua area and secure supply routes to the area. Troop strength was to be increased and preparations made for a resumption of offensive operations against Port Moresby.

Air operations were an essential part of this revised strategy. The IJNAF and IJAAF were ordered to rapidly reinforce their air strength and greatly expand air operations. Both services were expected to cooperate more closely to reduce Allied air strength, strike Allied supply routes, and protect Japanese supply routes. Within this new framework, air operations were also divided into areas of responsibility. The IJAAF principally focused on operations over New Guinea, and the IJNAF, while still engaged over New Guinea, shifted its main efforts to air defense of New Britain and New Ireland and air operations in the Solomons.

The detection of the Allied force build-up and the construction of new airbases in the New Guinea highlands prompted 8th Area Army at Rabaul to formulate new operational plans on June 20. In addition to completing strong defensive positions in the Lae–Salamaua area, an offensive against Wau was contemplated. The 6th Air Division was ordered to begin immediate attacks on the Allied airfields in the New Guinea highlands and against Oro Bay and Allied small craft moving along the New Guinea coast. The Allied landing at Nassau Bay, some ten miles south of Salamaua, on June 30, achieved tactical surprise, and despite 6th Air Division efforts, the Allies continued to pour new troops ashore. The Japanese decided to fight a decisive battle for Salamaua since loss of that base would render defense of Lae, some 25 miles to the north, untenable.

Under a July 4, 1943, agreement between 8th Area Army and Southeast Area Fleet, some 6th Air Division assets were temporarily shifted to the central Solomons. This left 6th Air Division unable to assist planned IJA attacks on Allied airstrips discovered in the

An IJAAF Dinah readies to depart on a reconnaissance mission from Lakunai. Reconnaissance was perhaps the most effective aspect of the IJAAF's defensive campaign. But while it detected the Allied construction of several airstrips in the New Guinea highlands in mid-1943 it missed the key construction site at Tsili Tsili until August. (AC)

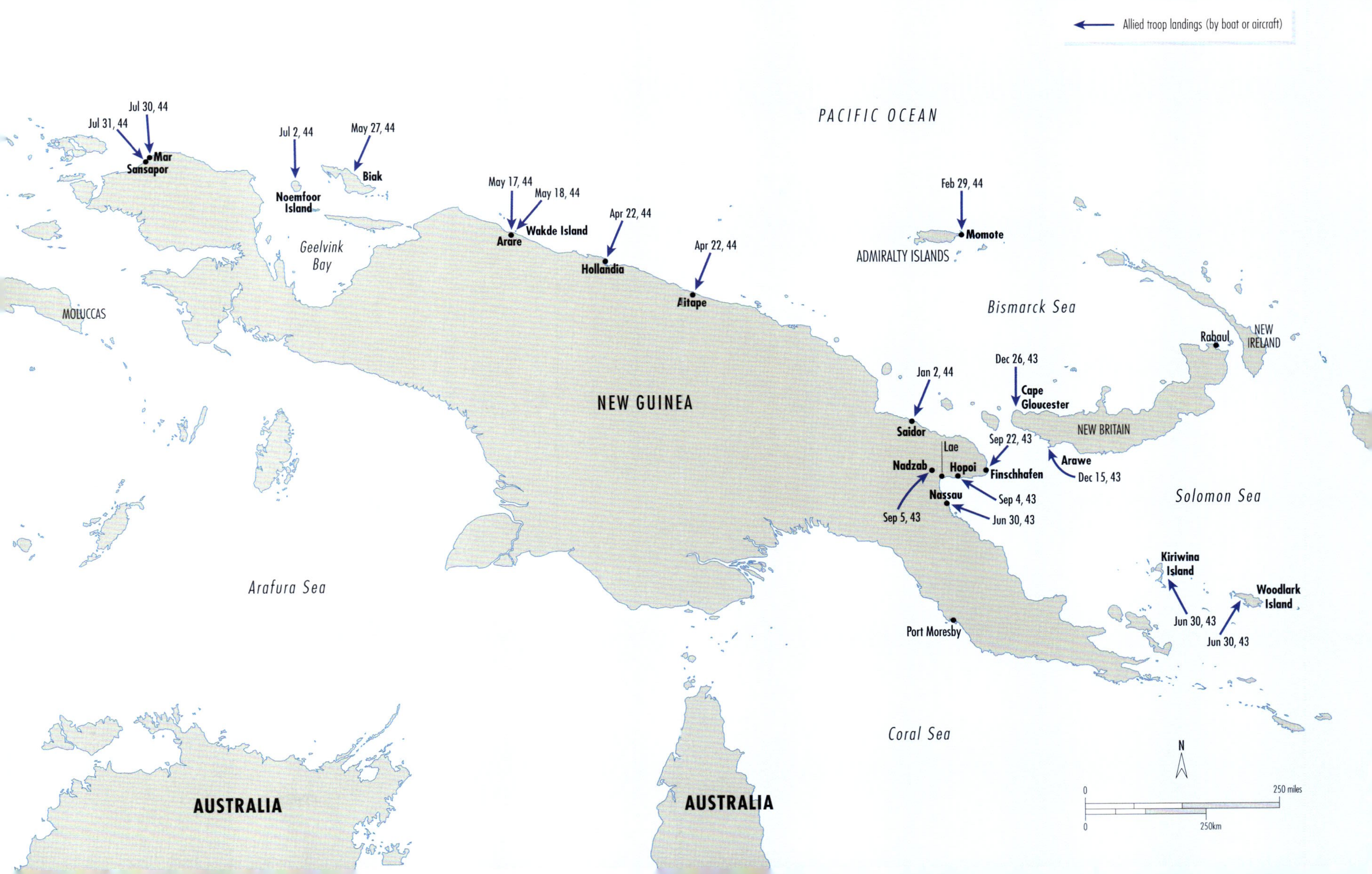

Allied troop landings (by boat or aircraft)
PACIFIC OCEAN
Jul 30, 44
Jul 31, 44
Mar
Sansapor
Jul 2, 44
Noemfoor Island
May 27, 44
Biak
Geelvink Bay
MOLUCCAS
May 17, 44
May 18, 44
Wakde Island
Arare
Apr 22, 44
Hollandia
Apr 22, 44
Aitape
Feb 29, 44
Momote
ADMIRALTY ISLANDS
Bismarck Sea
Rabaul
NEW IRELAND
Dec 26, 43
Cape Gloucester
NEW BRITAIN
Jan 2, 44
Saidor
NEW GUINEA
Lae
Sep 22, 43
Nadzab
Hopoi
Finschhafen
Arawe
Dec 15, 43
Nassau
Sep 4, 43
Sep 5, 43
Jun 30, 43
Solomon Sea
Kiriwina Island
Woodlark Island
Jun 30, 43
Jun 30, 43
Port Moresby
Arafura Sea
Coral Sea
N
0
250 miles
0
250km
AUSTRALIA
AUSTRALIA

New Guinea highlands. After successful USAAF attacks on Wewak the IJAAF was forced on the defensive and air support to IJA ground operations was severely reduced. More importantly, the movement of men and supplies by sea was seriously disrupted as it was much more difficult to provide air cover for land and maritime supply operations.

As their position continued to deteriorate, the Japanese were again forced to revise their strategy. On August 30, a new Army–Navy Central Agreement directed forces at Lae–Salamaua to conduct holding operations while new defensive positions were established to guard the Dampier Strait. But the Allies moved faster than the Japanese anticipated, and the IJA decided to evacuate Salamaua to reinforce Lae. The condition of the Lae garrison was greatly impacted by the inability to get supplies through the Allied air blockade. With no hope of holding out, the Lae garrison began to evacuate on September 12.

Being thrown on the defensive in New Guinea, and in the central Solomons, forced a fundamental revision of the IGHQ's strategy for the entire Pacific War. Given the shortage of ground forces and a growing Allied superiority in the air, the decision was made to fall back to the Empire's inner defenses and establish an "absolute zone of national defense" running from western New Guinea to the Mariana Islands, and a new 2nd Area Army was established in November 1943 at Davao in the Philippines to take control of operations in western New Guinea. Japanese positions in eastern New Guinea, New Britain, and New Ireland now constituted an outpost line.

Within this new strategy, Gen. Imamura ordered his 8th Area Army to perform its mission of strategic delay by launching counterattacks on all Allied efforts to penetrate the outpost perimeter. The Vitiaz and Dampier Straits were the focus of this defensive effort; the Japanese believed that if they could hold the straits, Allied advances into western New Guinea could be stopped. The 4th Air Army, headquartered at Wewak, was ordered to concentrate its aircraft on bases between Madang and Hollandia. Its primary mission became the destruction of Allied landing attempts in the straits region.

The Allies quickly followed up their success at Lae. On September 22, the Allies landed some five miles north of Finschhafen against no opposition, and occupied Finschhafen on October 2. On October 16, the Japanese launched a ground counterattack against the Allied beachhead and seemed poised to regain Finschhafen. Lack of supplies and the arrival of American reinforcements thwarted the attack, but the Japanese planned another attempt in November. Before their attack could begin, the Americans attacked on November 16. Heavy fighting resulted, and although 6th Air Division committed aircraft on ground support missions in late November, they could not stem the Allied advance. By December 17, the Japanese admitted defeat on the Huon Peninsula and ordered a retreat.

The series of attacks by 5th Air Force against Hollandia, Cyclops, and Sentani airfields in March and April 1944 effectively eliminated 4th Air Army as a force on New Guinea. Many aircrew and ground crew were afterwards forced to retreat west on foot. Here, a destroyed Tony sits at Cyclops airfield. (MacArthur Memorial)

Sio was the only important IJA defensive position between Allied forces driving up from Finschhafen and the important Japanese base at Madang. Again, the Japanese were surprised when on January 2, 1944, the Allies landed in the area of Saidor, about halfway between Sio and Madang. This move split 18th Army in half. Japan's outpost line had been shattered and the Allied offensive moved closer to the absolute defense zone. Both the IJA and IJN agreed that the pivotal factor for future operations was air power. Plans were made for constructing a large number of airfields, mutually supporting and echeloned in depth. In western New Guinea and the adjoining areas of the NEI only 27 airfields existed, and plans called for the construction of 96 new and the completion of seven more already partially built, for a total of 120, by the spring of 1944. The 2nd Area Army established key defense areas in the Sarmi–Wakde area and on Biak Island. This left the coast between Wewak and Sarmi–Wakde practically undefended. Included in this area was the important base at Hollandia.

The ambitious airfield construction program in the western New Guinea–NEI region fell seriously behind schedule. Of the 35 new airfields planned for western New Guinea, only nine were available by the end of April 1944. Similar problems were encountered trying to build up Japanese air power. The IJNAF's 1st Air Fleet units, earmarked for the defense zone, deployed from Japan to the Marianas in February instead of the NEI and New Guinea, and most of the remaining IJAAF air power in northeast New Guinea, 6th Air Division and 14th Air Brigade, were destroyed in the heavy March to April American strikes on Wewak and Hollandia. This set the stage for the Allied landings at Hollandia and Aitape on April 22 and the capture of the Japanese airfields at these locations. The loss of Hollandia compromised Japanese capability to defend western New Guinea, and IGHQ was forced once again to reconsider its strategy. On May 9, 1944, it directed that the defense line in western New Guinea be contracted so as to extend from Sorong to Halmahera.

However, as these plans were being finalized, the Americans seized Wakde on May 18, which was the forward defense for the Geelvink Bay area, including Biak, the keystone of Japanese defenses in western New Guinea. The Japanese made a concerted effort to hold Biak after the American landing on May 27. But Japanese air power in New Guinea was inadequate, and a series of attacks against Allied assault shipping caused no significant damage in exchange for heavy losses. The IJN planned to send its two largest warships to join the operation to land reinforcements on Biak, but when the Americans attacked Saipan in the Marianas on June 11, IGHQ essentially abandoned New Guinea.

THE CAMPAIGN

During the campaign, the Allies consistently targeted airfields to suppress Japanese air opposition to their westward momentum. Here a 500th Bomb Squadron B-25G participates in a May 11, 1944, attack on Wakde airstrip after it was pounded by B-24s of the 22nd Bomb Group. The Allies seized the airstrip exactly one week later. (NARA)

Build-up to the Allied offensive

Although Kenney had masterfully directed Allied air power during the expulsion of the Japanese from Papua, by May 1943 both 5th Air Force and RAAF Command were barely strong enough to maintain the status quo against the IJNAF and IJAAF forces arrayed against them. The USAAF inventory was in some ways worse than it had been in late 1942, totaling 565 fighters and bombers on paper, but substantially fewer operationally. Some groups were low on serviceable aircraft or had none operational, and some units were out of action while transitioning to newer aircraft. For example, the whole 22nd Bomb Group was refitting in Australia. The 90th Bomb Group's 319th Bomb Squadron had been deployed to NWA since February 1943 to provide additional reconnaissance and striking power against Japanese air and naval bases in the NEI and western New Guinea, and thus was unavailable for operations in eastern New Guinea. The 380th Bomb Group, newly arrived with B-24Ds and slated for NWA basing, was just getting acclimated in May to theater operations. Some of its aircraft flew alongside the 43rd Bomb Group from Port Moresby while others joined the 319th Bomb Squadron in Australia. Some of the 317th Troop Carrier Group's C-47s were unavailable, working in Australia with the Directorate for Air Transport, and the six Douglas P-70s of the 6th Night Fighter Squadron that arrived in March to defend Port Moresby proved to be inadequate. Although Kenney had negotiated successfully with the JCS for additional reinforcements, these would only arrive in staggered fashion during mid- to late-1943.

The RAAF also had problems. Of its 31 squadrons assigned to Allied Air Forces, seven were assigned directly to 5th Air Force within No 9 Operational Group and the remainder fell under Bostock's RAAF Command. As of May, the RAAF had 1,441 aircraft of all types, but only 689 (48 percent) were serviceable. The RAAF was also short of trained personnel; No 9 Group was short of about 1,695 personnel in May and over 2,000 by July. This personnel shortage plagued the RAAF throughout the campaign. The RAAF could also expect during 1943 only a trickle of additional American aircraft – 34 Vengeances, 60 Kittyhawks, and 12 Catalinas.

The threat from Rabaul loomed large and the March 28 JCS directive required Kenney to defend MacArthur's "right" flank by first advancing the Allies' "bomber line" against Rabaul while dealing with IJA strongholds along New Guinea's northern coast. While the Allies already operated from Milne Bay and the RAAF had Vivigani airstrip on Goodenough Island in use by May 17, *Elkton III* called for shoring up Allied air power at the eastern end of New Guinea by occupying Woodlark and Kiriwina Islands on June 30 to acquire fighter bases for escorting bombers in daylight to Rabaul. Both Kenney and Hewitt were anxious to consolidate RAAF air power in eastern New Guinea for it to play a significant role in operations against Rabaul. Therefore, as soon as practicable, No 9 Operational Group was to move its bomber and fighter squadrons to the new airfields. This would facilitate mission planning and execution with 5th Air Force operations, especially with V Fighter Command squadrons at Dobodura. Meanwhile, the forces in NWA, and to a lesser extent in NEA, covering the "left" flank of MacArthur's campaign, would maintain pressure on the Japanese, forcing them to defend the NEI and limiting their build-up in western New Guinea. The USAAF 319th Bomb Squadron and RAAF Nos 2, 18, and 31 Squadrons were able to take the fight to the Japanese in the NEI by May.

As the IJAAF and IJNAF implemented the March 1943 Army–Navy Central Agreement, they estimated Allied air strength in May at 250 combat aircraft at Port Moresby, 100 at Dobodura, and 100 at Milne Bay. Gen. Imamura viewed 18th Army's situation in New Guinea as serious and directed that 4th Air Army, stood up in April, establish its headquarters at Wewak between June and August. The 6th Air Division had already stationed some of its units at New Guinea airfields over the preceding two months. The IJAAF 7th Air Division would arrive in June with two thirds of its forces, leaving the rest at Ambon in the NEI. Of the IJAAF aircraft already in the theater, about one third were left in the Rabaul area by early August, while the remainder constituted the New Guinea build-up. This included the Hakujoshi Operational Training Air Brigade's 45th and 208th Air Regiments' Lilys and most of the 14th Air Regiment's Sallys as the core of 4th Air Army's offensive capability. Supporting these bombers were the Oscars of the 1st, 11th and 24th Air Regiments, the Tonys of the 68th Air Regiment, and the Nicks of the 13th Air Regiment. Rabaul-area airfields at Lakunai, Vunakanau, and Rapopo also hosted significant IJNAF 25th and 26th Air Flotilla forces. In the NEI, the IJAAF 3rd Air Army had the 61st Air Regiment equipped with Helens, the 75th Air Regiment with Lilys, the 5th Air Regiment with Nicks, and the 59th Air Regiment flying Oscars, while the IJNAF's

A 14th Air Regiment Sally flies over the New Guinea jungle, October 1943. The IJAAF classified the Sally as a "heavy" bomber. The 14th was a key part of 4th Air Army's effort to strike back at the advancing Allied air power, flying both day and night missions. (NARA)

23rd Air Flotilla was comprised of the 202 Air Group flying Zeros, the 753 Air Group equipped with Bettys, and various seaplanes of 934 Air Group to threaten New Guinea and Australia.

Encircling Rabaul and isolating New Guinea

By May, the Japanese had implemented a new strategy for resupplying their front-line garrisons on New Guinea. After the debacles of the Buna and Lae maritime resupply efforts from November 1942 to March 1943, the Japanese ceased using destroyers and very large transports in the immediate combat zone, switching to what a senior IJNAF staff officer at Rabaul called a "scrabbler's run" of smaller transports and barges from New Britain and NEI along with occasional deliveries by submarines. The Allies responded by increasing intelligence collection on maritime supply traffic. This required increased reconnaissance sorties by both heavy and medium bombers, usually singly but sometimes in twos and threes, dedicated to armed reconnaissance ("recco" in SWPA parlance). Bomber squadrons flew recco missions throughout 1943 until more dedicated long-range reconnaissance units arrived. Each mission usually lasted several hours during which aircraft gathered information and attacked targets of opportunity on land or at sea. Information was passed in-flight by trailing a 200ft antenna for HF radio communication with ADVON. However, this left fewer aircraft and crews for pure bombing missions due to follow-up maintenance and crew rest requirements. Allied cracking of IJN and IJA operational ciphers related to transport movements provided invaluable assistance to recco missions.

Weather allowing, in the first half of May the USAAF flew several single heavy bomber reccos. These were often very dangerous missions. The 321st Bomb Squadron sent a B-24D recco north of New Britain on May 5 during which it made unsuccessful attacks against a "cruiser" and later a 2,500-ton transport due to bombs hanging up in its bomb bay. The B-24D was hit by antiaircraft fire from the transport that damaged fuel lines, but the bomber returned for a crash landing at Dobodura. The 63rd Bomb Squadron lost one B-17F recco on May 7 to six 253 Air Group Zeros while photographing suspected new construction near Kavieng, and the next day lost another B-17F while investigating two 500-ton transports enroute to Madang from Hansa Bay after it collided with one of three intercepting 11th Air Regiment Oscars. Keeping pressure on the Japanese supply system, on eight days between May 1 and 15, 43rd and 90th Bomb Group heavies bombed or strafed Japanese maritime supply traffic north of New Guinea and New Britain and docks at Finschhafen. Allied medium bomb groups were also very active against supply traffic. The two transports sighted by the 63rd recco off Madang on May 8 were sunk later that day by nine 3rd Bomb Group B-25C-1s and eight No 30 Squadron Beaufighters diverted from a strafing mission to Madang. Onboard those transports were food and personnel and the entire IJA 11th Airfield Construction Unit, an asset 4th Air Army could ill afford to lose. On May 15, First Air Task Force at Dobodura, tipped off by intercepted IJN radio communications, sent five 90th Bomb Squadron

Though RAAF No 30 Squadron flew mainly ground support around Salamaua early in the campaign, it also joined 5th Air Force in deeper attacks on Japanese shipping and airfields. On May 8, eight Beaufighters joined nine 90th Bomb Squadron B-25C-1s in attacking Madang, destroying this probable 11th Air Regiment Oscar. (NARA)

B-25Ds against a submarine making a nighttime supply delivery to Lae, with the damaged submarine reportedly departing without making its delivery.

During early May, while they intensified efforts to destroy Japanese maritime supply assets, the Allies flew continuous ground support sorties against 18th Army units in the Lae–Salamaua area. No 22 Squadron's Bostons were especially active in supporting the Australian 3rd Division against the IJA 51st Division. Wirraways of No 4 and Beaufighters of No 30 Squadrons, along with A-20Gs of the USAAF 89th Bomb Squadron, also provided support, while C-47s dropped needed supplies. Ground support requested by the 3rd Division, as during the Buna fighting in 1942, went through ADVON and was ordered from there or by the First Air Task Force. These missions were often a source of frustration for the flyers and supported troops alike; for the former due to their inability to see results of their attacks through the dense jungle cover and for the latter due to the difficulty in coordinating their troop movements with close air attacks. However, the ground fighting at this time was essentially a holding action to keep just enough pressure on Japanese ground forces to convince 18th Army's command that Salamaua, not Lae, was the Allies' next objective.

The Allies also maintained pressure on Rabaul and redoubled efforts to suppress other Japanese airfields closest to their upcoming ground offensive. The Wewak, Madang, Cape Gloucester, and Gasmata areas were prime Allied targets. Rabaul and its airfields were targeted five times in the first half of May. All missions were flown at night. The May 8 mission saw four 64th Bomb Squadron B-17Fs drop incendiaries on Vunakanau, starting several small fires. On the 11th, weather interfered and only six 65th Bomb Squadron B-17Fs and two 400th Bomb Squadron B-24Ds managed to hit Vunakanau again, possibly destroying some aircraft on the runway based on where fires were observed. May 13 through 15 saw raids each night by 43rd Bomb Group B-17Fs hitting Vunakanau and Lakunai. During two of these missions crews reported that some Rabaul antiaircraft fire, which did no damage, consisted of "fireworks" rounds that rose like rockets, burst at altitude and shot out brilliant filaments. These were very likely prototype IJN Type 4 *RoSa-dan* incendiary rockets that each discharged 24 incendiary fragments. Airfields at Gasmata, Lae, Cape Gloucester (Tuluvu), Madang, and Wewak were hit multiple times day and night by small numbers of both heavy and medium bombers. Gasmata was bombed and strafed nine times through May 15, mostly by medium bombers, and was essentially put out of action while the others sustained only minor damage. Rare good weather allowed a relatively large strike against Madang airfield and village on May 7 by the 65th and 320th Bomb Squadrons just after daybreak. Six aircraft from each squadron dropped 300lb wire-wrapped "daisy cutter" bombs from 3,500ft to 5,500ft through relatively heavy antiaircraft fire that damaged several attackers. Some storage facilities were also set afire.

Because the Allies could not consistently cover the westernmost high-priority targets such as Wewak, they began searching for locations to build or improve airfields closer to these objectives. This search led initially to a small pre-war grass airstrip called Marilinan, but due to soil composition it was only suitable for transport and some fighter operations. This led to a decision in early June to build an airstrip five miles southwest, about 50 miles west of Lae at Tsili Tsili (Kenney, who disliked the name, continued to call it "Marilinan"). Tsili Tsili was only usable during the dry season, which ended around September, but it would

During the campaign No 22 Squadron's Bostons both supported Allied ground forces and hunted Japanese supply barges in New Guinea and New Britain. Here a Boston III aircrewman disembarks after a mission in December 1943. This particular Boston was reportedly one of only two modified to carry twin .303in tail machine guns. (AWM)

serve in the interim until Nadzab, previously identified by the Australians as suitable for an airfield, could be developed. The Tsili Tsili airfield work proceeded during June and July in secrecy, greatly aided by local workers, who made a big show of the construction of smaller emergency and supply airstrips northwest of Tsili Tsili and south-southwest of Madang to divert IJAAF attention. These locations included Bena Bena, Goroka (Garoka), Mt. Hagan, and Kainantu. The 8th Area Army became aware of this diversionary construction activity through aerial reconnaissance in June and understood the threat that Allied airfields in the area represented to 18th Army positions in both the Huon Peninsula and on the coast. The IJAAF began bombing raids against these locations almost immediately, and 8th Area Army planned to deploy troops to seize Bena Bena at the earliest opportunity. Work at Tsili Tsili, meanwhile, went on unobserved.

The beginning of the Allies' aerial offensive in early May was easier due to the lack of Japanese pressure over New Guinea in the wake of losses from the unsuccessful *I-Go* operations in April. Allied fighter units assumed a routine of flying mostly transport escort and patrol missions. However, on May 13, the Japanese resumed air raids on New Guinea targets. That evening, a 251 Air Group Irving flew reconnaissance over Dobodura, probably seeking intelligence on a large Allied supply convoy heading for Oro Bay, and five unidentified IJNAF aircraft scattered bombs in the Dobodura area and two on Port Moresby without causing damage. The next day, preceded by a Dinah reconnaissance flight, 33 251 Air Group Zeros escorted 18 751 Air Group Bettys to hit the Oro Bay supply convoy, reaching their target about 1010hrs. However, the Allies' own May 13 reconnaissance had revealed 113 fighters and 84 bombers at Rabaul airfields (hence their nighttime heavy bomber attacks mentioned above) and ADVON alerted the entire 49th Fighter Group at Dobodura that evening to expect a Japanese attack next day. Thus, on May 14, the first large-scale air battle in more than a month developed over Oro Bay as the 49th's 13 P-38s and 26 P-40s tangled with the Zeros as the Bettys bombed transports and the dock area from about 17,000ft. The 45-minute encounter resulted in limited damage to Allied supply transports, communications lines between Oro Bay and Dobodura, and a fuel dump. One 9th Squadron P-38G was shot down with the pilot killed and one 7th Fighter Squadron P-40K was written off after crash landing at Dobodura; six Bettys were lost and the remainder received damage. The 49th claimed ten Zeros destroyed, but IJNAF records showed all returned to base.

A 41st Fighter Squadron P-39K. As the campaign began the 40th and 41st Fighter Squadrons flew P-39s from 12-Mile (Berry/Bomana) 'Drome near Port Moresby in base defense, transport escort, and ground support missions. In late July they began moving to Tsili Tsili and countered the IJAAF attack on August 15, 1943. (NARA)

Over the rest of May, the IJAAF and IJNAF followed up with both night raids on Dobodura and Port Moresby on May 15, 18, and 19 and daylight attacks on Wau and Allied positions in the ground fighting around Salamaua on May 17, 19, and 21, sometimes using Lae as a staging base. On May 15, the 208th Air Regiment flew its first combat mission in New Guinea, as its Lilys, escorted by 11th Air Regiment Oscars, tried to attack New Guinea Force positions near Salamaua but hit IJA positions instead. Also, on the night of May 15, a 14th Air Regiment Sally, flying from Rabaul, was shot down by the 6th Night Fighter Squadron as it raided Seven-Mile 'Drome at Port Moresby. This was the only kill by the 6th of the campaign and the P-70 was lucky to avoid being hit itself by Allied antiaircraft fire. Eleven 80th Fighter Squadron P-38s escorting C-47s to Wau on May 21 were diverted to Salamaua and encountered 15–20 1st or 11th Air Regiment Oscars, themselves escorting bombers. The Americans claimed six Japanese fighters for no loss. The Japanese were also busy dropping supplies to their troops fighting around Salamaua and to units engaged in road building further west. Such air activity told the Allies that more IJAAF airfields were becoming operational further west and that Japanese aerial opposition was likely to increase. The Allies were kept apprised of the enemy aircraft build-up by photographic evidence available from 8th Photo Reconnaissance Squadron F-4s flying as far west as Wewak and F-5s that could reach New Ireland, through tactical communications intercepts, and through ULTRA. By these means the Allies learned of the presence of the 45th Air Regiment (Lilys) at Rabaul in

Tho IJNAF introduced dedicated night fighters into the theater in May 1943 when modified Nakajima J1N1-S Irvings joined 251 Air Group at Lakunai. Armed with two angled, forward-firing dorsal and two ventral 20mm cannon, Irvings accounted for a few Allied bomber losses, but withdrew to Truk by early February 1944. (AC)

Opening shots

The lull in Japanese attacks on New Guinea that occurred after the conclusion of *I-Go* in April ended on May 14, 1943, when the IJNAF decided to strike a large Allied supply convoy due to dock in Oro Bay that day. Eighteen 751 Air Group Bettys from Kavieng, escorted by 32 251 Air Group Zeros, appeared at 1010hrs at 17,000ft in the vicinity of their target in unusually clear skies. The Allied warning network alerted all three 49th Fighter Group squadrons and they were airborne well before the Japanese appeared. In a 45 minute battle 26 P-40s and 13 P-38s intercepted the Bettys near their target, the 8th diving from 20,000ft out of the sun to attack. The 7th followed immediately behind from 22,000ft. Just before being attacked the Bettys proceeded to bomb the shipping and pier area. After setting fire to a fuel dump and causing other minor damage the Bettys turned northeast for home. As the P-40s attacked them from the port rear quarter the Zeros fell upon the P-40s and a dogfight ensued. Another P-40 element attacked the Bettys head on. Seven 9th Squadron P-38s arrived from 24,000ft as the initial dogfight started but only one managed to fire on the Bettys before becoming embroiled in the dogfight with the Zeros. One P-38G was shot down and the pilot was seen to parachute over water but later no sign of him was found. Four P-38s arriving a bit later chased the Bettys farther out to sea and damaged one but were then cut off by Zeros and returned to base. In total the 751 Air Group lost six Bettys while the 251 Air Group Zeros, in addition to shooting down the P-38G, damaged a 7th Squadron P-40K severely enough that it was a write-off upon crash landing at Dobodura.

313
37
K-327
K-310

Jim Laurier

mid-May, and that the 24th Air Regiment (Oscars) was at But and Dagua (But East) by late May. The Oscars, in fact, began flying defensive sorties in early May, claiming five B-24Ds downed during the month with only one actually lost.

These and additional Japanese aircraft movements increased the threat from both Rabaul and Wewak. In response, during the latter half of May, the Allies increased the tempo of operations. Rabaul came in for attention three more times and Kavieng once, but there was a new wrinkle to these night missions. When six 64th Bomb Squadron B-17s hit various Rabaul-area targets on May 21 at about 0300hrs, setting fires at presumed ammunition dumps, two B-17Es were lost to an IJNAF Irving night fighter. Newly introduced into the theater with 251 Air Group at Lakunai, about nine Irvings would operate from Rabaul for the remainder of the year, usually singly but sometimes in pairs, and in conjunction with searchlights since they carried no radar.

During the same period, the Allies also kept up the pressure on other critical locations. Airfields and supply dumps on New Britain received the most attention. Gasmata was struck at least 11 times and Cape Gloucester three times. Allied sorties against Gasmata and Cape Gloucester comprised B-25s (62), A-20s (17), B-17s (7), B-24s (15), Beaufighters (18), and Beauforts (15). Additionally, Madang was hit four times, Lae–Salamaua and Finschhafen three, and Wewak and Saidor twice each. While each raid involved only a few Allied aircraft and inflicted only minor damage, they did serve to disrupt Japanese operations. Meanwhile, RAAF Hudsons and Beauforts at Milne Bay performed important reconnaissance over the Solomon Sea as preparations for the initial *Cartwheel* operations ramped up.

Air war on the "left" flank

Elkton III required that any Japanese incursions into the Arafura Sea–Torres Strait area be blocked, and, if necessary, the Australian 11th Brigade garrison at Merauke be reinforced by air. On May 20, Bostock directed Bladin to harass Japanese forces in western New Guinea and the NEI both to guard SWPA's southern flank and to keep them guessing whether, or not, the Allies were planning an amphibious offensive from Australia. This entailed hunting Japanese supply transports and hitting any airfields in the NEI and New Guinea used by the IJAAF and IJNAF for attacking Australia and defending key infrastructure. Since February 1943, the 319th Bomb Squadron at Fenton had provided long-range reconnaissance and strike options, and the arrival of the 380th Bomb Group's four B-24D squadrons in NWA between April and June to relieve the 319th further bolstered NWA's long-range capability; the 319th rejoined the 90th Bomb Group at Five-Mile 'Drome in July. Air Cmdre Cobby's NEA also supported the effort by assigning No 84 Squadron Boomerangs at Horn Island patrol duty over Merauke. Development of additional airfields began at Merauke, and at Millingimbi and other northern Australian locations.

A 319th Bomb Squadron B-24D takes off from Fenton in NWA. Kenney stationed first 90th and later 380th Bomb Group B-24s in NWA to provide longer-range strike and reconnaissance capabilities to the theater's southern flank. These B-24s greatly disrupted Japanese efforts to support the IJAAF in New Guinea throughout the campaign. (AWM)

The IJNAF 23rd Air Flotilla at Kendari had primary responsibility for the area west and southwest of New Guinea. Its missions included convoy escort, defense of the Celebes, reconnaissance of the Arafura and Timor Seas, and "monthly" attacks on Darwin and Merauke. The flotilla's 934 Air Group fighter and reconnaissance seaplanes flew from bases in the Arafura Sea and on New Guinea. The IJAAF 7th Air Division assisted the 23rd from bases at Ambon, Lautem and Penfui in the NEI and was responsible for western New Guinea, operating mostly from Sorong, Kamiri,

Babo, Wakde, and Mokmer (Biak). The IJAAF also undertook, at this time, to build or improve additional airfields in western New Guinea.

No 18 Squadron was the only Dutch unit involved in the campaign. Flying from McDonald in NWA its B-25s, crewed by both Dutch and Australians, constantly attacked Japanese airfields and marine transports operating in western New Guinea and the NEI. Its aircraft had converted mainly to strafers by mid-1943. (AWM)

Radar support provided by No 38 Radar Station at Cape Fourcroy on Bathurst Island, just off the coast from Darwin, enabled NWA air units to blunt 7th Air Division and 23rd Air Flotilla attacks on Australia and southern New Guinea. During nineteen days in May, the aggressive Bladin launched strikes on key Japanese airfields and naval facilities in western New Guinea and the NEI. Targets included Manokwari, Babo, Kaimana, and Nabire in western New Guinea, and NEI locations such as Penfui, Koepang, Dili, and Kendari. The 319th Bomb Squadron's B-24Ds, joined by some newly arrived aircraft of the 528th Bomb Squadron, hit mainly New Guinea targets, while the Dutch No 18 Squadron's B-25Cs carried out a large share of night raids against Penfui and Dili on Timor. June saw the first raid by the entire 380th Bomb Group when, on the 11th, its four squadrons hit naval and air facilities at Koepang from around 9,000ft. Zeros of 202 Air Group intercepted and three B-24Ds were lost, one of which was a "ferret" carrying an Australian sergeant from the RAAF's secretive Section 22 tasked to collect Japanese radar signal data. Additional Allied raids in late June included No 31 Squadron Beaufighters hitting the 75th Air Regiment at the new airfield at Selaru in the Tanimbar Islands and 17 528th Bomb Squadron B-24Ds bombing Makassar (Macassar) by day, losing one bomber in a collision with a defending Zero.

The RAAF's 1st Fighter Wing defending NWA, however, initially performed poorly. Several Japanese night sorties against Australia went completely unchallenged, while a big IJNAF May 2 daylight attack on Darwin highlighted the inexperienced wing's poor tactics and situational awareness. That morning, 33 Spitfire Vs of the wing's three Spitfire squadrons (No 54 RAF, Nos 452 and 457 RAAF) got the worst of a running fight with 25 753 Air Group Bettys escorted by 27 202 Air Group Zeros that flew from Penfui to bomb Darwin's Winnellie airfield. The Japanese reported only six Bettys damaged. Their raid caused negligible damage, but NWA had lost two pilots killed and 12 Spitfires. Five were lost in combat with the remainder through mechanical malfunctions or fuel depletion. The Spitfire squadrons had spent precious time and fuel trying to form up inexperienced pilots to attack as a wing rather than engaging the Japanese in smaller elements at the earliest opportunity. NWA fighters thereafter carried 30gal drop tanks, when available, and gradually changed policy to avoid dogfighting and to intercept enemy bombers at the earliest opportunity. Spitfires gave somewhat better accounts of themselves against IJNAF attacks targeting Millingimbi on May 10, 13, and 28, shooting down six while losing only three.

On June 20, the IJAAF got involved with a well-coordinated high/low altitude attack against the Darwin area. Escorted by 22 59th Air Regiment Oscars, 18 61st Air Regiment Helens flew at about 25,000ft and bombed Winnellie airfield, hitting huts, cutting a railroad line, and destroying a railcar loaded with fuel drums. Meanwhile, nine Lilys of the 75th Air Regiment, fitted with auxiliary fuel tanks, flew at between 100ft and 200ft altitude and hit Winnellie, first with bombs and in a second sweep with machine gun fire. They hit supply dumps, antiaircraft positions, and No 54 Squadron facilities. Nos 452, 457, and 54 Squadrons conducted a creditable defense and accounted for at least three Helens, three Lilys and two Oscars for the loss of two Spitfires. But this was the only IJAAF raid of its kind; the 75th attacked NWA only once more in September. The 61st also only raided

Gun camera frame showing a No 452 Squadron Spitfire Vb's attack on one of 26 753 Air Group Bettys raiding the 380th Bomb Group's NWA Fenton base on July 6, 1943. During this raid four Bettys were destroyed and 13 damaged, leading 23rd Air Flotilla to discontinue daylight attacks on Australia. (AWM)

NWA two additional times before transferring to New Guinea in September, and a stream of IJAAF units followed them to New Guinea through the following March.

The IJNAF made additional major attacks on Australia in late June and early July. Aircraft from the 23rd Air Flotilla mounted major raids on June 28 and 30, and July 6, including on its target list the newly arrived 380th Bomb Group. On June 28 and 30, 753 Air Group Bettys escorted by 202 Air Group Zeros attacked Fenton. The attack on the 30th saw 23 Bettys and 23 Zeros at about 25,000ft engaged with 31 Spitfires at around noon. Defending Spitfires again spent valuable time and fuel massing for a frontal attack and thus could make only one ineffective pass before the bombers dropped 150 bombs. On this occasion, the bombing was accurate and destroyed three B-24Ds and damaged seven, along with other equipment at the airfield. In addition to its steep tactical learning curve, 1st Wing fighters suffered many engine and weapons failures that also reduced their effectiveness. Losses to 1st Wing were four Spitfires shot down and two damaged in combat, and three lost due to mechanical problems; two pilots were killed. In return, the 23rd Air Flotilla suffered three Bettys crash landed or written off due to damage. July 6 saw 26 Bettys and 21 Zeros again head for Fenton. From 29,000ft they dropped 140 bombs at about 1200hrs on the dispersal area, destroying one B-24D and damaging three more along with several antiaircraft guns. During the 35-minute battle, 33 intercepting Spitfires shot down two Bettys. Two more were written off in crash landings while 13 sustained lesser battle damage. Five Spitfires were lost with two pilots killed. This was the last daylight IJNAF raid on Australia. Over the next several months the 23rd Air Flotilla saw many of its aircraft and best pilots siphoned off by the 25th Air Flotilla at Rabaul to vanish into the Solomons meat grinder.

New Guinea also came under occasional attack by 23rd Air Flotilla. On September 9, RAAF No 316 Radar Station at Cape Kombies, 120 miles west of Merauke, reported an IJNAF raid at about 1000hrs inbound to Merauke. Fourteen NEA No 86 Squadron Kittyhawks, stationed at Merauke since June 30, launched to meet the raid along with four No 84 Squadron Boomerangs. The Kittyhawks attacked the Japanese formation of 16 Bettys and 16 Zeros at 20,000ft, however all but four Kittyhawks suffered gun problems, and the Boomerangs never reached the Japanese formation. Nevertheless, No 86 claimed three Zeros for no losses. The Bettys holed the airstrip and destroyed one Boomerang on the ground, but overall the damage was minor. Thereafter, mainly due to the steady decrease of 23rd Air Flotilla power mentioned above, most air combat in the Arafura Sea–Torres Strait region was confined to exchanges between various RAAF aircraft and 934 Air Group floatplanes stationed mainly at Taberfane in the Aru Islands.

Operation *Cartwheel* opens

In June, during the lead-up to the initial *Cartwheel* operations, the Allies continued their main air effort against Japanese Huon Peninsula positions. Troop locations and airfields at Lae and Salamaua were hit a total of 13 times in June by heavy and medium bombers, along with other locations such as Finschhafen and area coastal transport traffic. Ahead of the upcoming SWPA landings on Woodlark and Kiriwina Islands

(Operation *Chronicle*) and SOPAC's assault on New Georgia, Rabaul airfields were subjected to night attacks by the 43rd and 90th Bomb Groups, with some 380th Bomb Group support as some of their crews gained experience before moving to NWA. As weather allowed, Rabaul raids were flown on June 3, 10–11, 13–15, 19–20, 26, and 30, usually with unobserved results. During these missions, Irving night fighters claimed six victories and two probables on five interceptions; in fact, the 43rd lost four B-17s. The 4th Air Army responded with ground support missions by the 14th, 45th, and 208th Air Regiments in the Huon Peninsula area and mounted nuisance raids on Port Moresby and Dobodura. Japanese aircraft also frequently raided Wau and the Allied airstrips (real and diversionary) under construction in the New Guinea highlands as Japanese reconnaissance "discovered" them. The first of such raids occurred on June 14 when, escorted by Oscars, 14th Air Regiment Sallys struck Bena Bena while 208th Air Regiment Lilys hit Kainantu. The 4th Air Army mounted similar attacks again on June 16 and periodically thereafter.

An 80th Fighter Squadron P-38G gets maintenance in a revetment at Port Moresby's Three-Mile (Kila) 'Drome on September 14, 1943. The squadron was involved in many major air battles throughout the campaign. The 80th retained its P-38s when the 475th Fighter Group stood up, unlike the 9th and 39th Fighter Squadrons. (NARA)

During June there were only two significant air engagements. On June 12, nine 9th Fighter Squadron P-38s dueled eight 1st Air Regiment Oscars near Bena Bena, claiming two for no losses. On June 21, 14 80th Fighter Squadron P-38s escorted five 501st Bomb Squadron B-25Ds to drop supplies to Australian 3rd Division elements southwest of Salamaua – the first mission flown by the newly arrived 345th Bomb Group. Alerted to Japanese fighters nearby by No 22 Squadron Bostons that were supporting troops in the same area, the 80th engaged 22 24th Air Regiment Oscars that had been escorting eight probable 208th Air Regiment Lilys attacking Australian positions. A wild melee ensued west of Lae ending with the Japanese claiming eight P-38s destroyed while the 80th claimed 13 kills and 10 probables; in fact, no P-38s were lost and the 24th only reported one pilot killed, though perhaps as many as six Oscars were downed.

The Milne Bay 'drome had two functioning airstrips, Gurney and Turnbull. RAAF Nos 6, 75, 77, and 100 Squadrons had used these facilities since May, conducting reconnaissance and area defense, as the Milne Bay base had been built into an important staging point for Allied troop and supply movements. The Allies expected strong Japanese attacks on Milne Bay as forces for *Chronicle* arrived, but these never materialized. Raids by the IJNAF were limited to sporadic nighttime attacks by single aircraft causing very limited damage. However, it still seemed prudent to send fighters to Milne Bay just ahead of the *Chronicle* landings, and some 39th and 80th Fighter Squadron P-38s staged to Milne Bay several days prior to June 30 to augment the RAAF units there. These initial SWPA amphibious operations saw the first of what became regular disagreements between Kenney and MacArthur's naval commanders. R. Adm. Barbey, in charge of the landings, was of the opinion that Allied Air Forces should fly aircraft over amphibious forces continuously, whereas Kenney thought that they should simply be available on ground alert to respond to incoming Japanese air attacks. On D-day Kenney won out, but in the event neither the Kiriwina nor Woodlark landing was contested by Japanese aircraft.

The Nassau Bay landing by the Americans on June 30 was preceded by almost daily area attacks by Bostons and, on June 29, by 89th Bomb Squadron A-20Gs hitting nearby IJA supply dumps. Weather over the landing area on June 30 was awful and neither side flew sorties related to the landing until July 2, when 10 unidentified Japanese bombers made bombing and strafing runs against Allied positions. The next afternoon, 13

OPPOSITE WEWAK-AREA AIRFIELDS

Wewak hosted 4th Air Army Headquarters and important airfields from which the IJAAF conducted its defensive effort.

The 54th Troop Carrier Wing's C-47s constantly moved men and material to support ground fighting and Allied air units that were leapfrogging to various bases. Here, a C-47 delivers much-needed supplies by parachute, probably ammunition, on August 1, 1943, to Allied troops fighting near Salamaua. (AWM)

7th Fighter Squadron P-40Ks returning from escorting C-47s supplying Australian troops spotted eight of 20 208th Air Regiment Lilys flying line astern at 3,000ft bombing the landing area. As the 7th turned to attack, it was met by 16 escorting 24th Air Regiment Oscars. In the 15-minute fight the P-40s probably downed four Oscars and a Lily for no losses. The supply situation for the American ground forces fighting their way to link up with the Australians was initially bad due to poor-to-nonexistent trails between the shore and combat areas inland, but C-47s managed to drop food, ammunition, and other essentials at specified locations to be gathered up by Allied troops.

Both the Allies and Japanese saw changes to their respective force structures during this period. For the Allies, the 345th Bomb Group's four squadrons of B-25Gs became fully operational in July at Port Moresby. The 19th Bomb Squadron, sporting its natural metal finished "Silver Fleet" B-26s, resumed New Guinea operations from Dobodura on July 21. Also in late July, the 348th Fighter Group's P-47Ds became operational from Port Moresby's Five- and Seven-Mile 'Dromes, while on August 12 the 475th Fighter Group's P-38s began operations from Five-, Seven-, and 12-Mile 'Dromes. The 375th Troop Carrier Group also initially joined the 54th Troop Carrier Wing at Port Moresby in early July, but within a month moved its C-47s to Dobodura under the First Air Task Force. In July, the RAAF's No 4 Squadron added Boomerangs to aid in ground support and, with the Vivigani strip on Goodenough Island already operational and the completion of two airstrips on Kiriwina on July 18, No 9 Operational Group's Beaufighters and Bostons prepared to move there from Port Moresby to join the fighters of Nos 75, 76, 77, and 79 Squadrons by mid-August.

The 4th Air Army bolstered its 6th Air Division forces already based in New Guinea with 7th Air Division units from the NEI. These included the 59th Air Regiment's Oscars in mid-July at But. Most of the 14th Air Brigade's 68th and 78th Air Regiments' Tonys moved from Rabaul to Boram (Wewak East) and Wewak, respectively, also by mid-July. The 7th Air Regiment's Helens reached Dagua on July 24. Reconnaissance units flying Dinahs and Sonias from the Wewak-area airfields, Madang and Alexishafen, included the 74th, 81st, and 83rd Independent Squadrons and two squadrons of the 10th Air Regiment. Meanwhile, the 1st Air Regiment withdrew from New Guinea in August. The 4th Air Army established its headquarters at Wewak by August 10, joining the 6th Air Division Headquarters that arrived there on July 9 and thereafter assuming sole responsibility for New Guinea air operations east of Hollandia, as per the March Army–Navy agreement.

The fighting intensified accordingly. Allied air power focused on preparations for Operation *Postern*, the seizure of Lae. Operations supporting ground forces fighting in the area south and west of Salamaua throughout July were the heaviest. No 4 Squadron's Boomerangs and Wirraways provided direct tactical support. The 5th's medium and heavy bombers flew more than 600 sorties against IJA forces whenever weather permitted, hitting targets on 28 days in July. Maritime supply traffic was also targeted by more than 100 medium bomber sorties in late July, with attacks on July 28 and 29 around

Cape Gloucester resulting in claims of two destroyers sunk and numerous barges destroyed. Three big raids between July 20 and 23 also hit the area around Madang and Bogadjim that the Allies identified as a burgeoning supply point. While the Lae–Salamaua and Madang areas saw the most consistent attacks, there were still sorties dedicated to maintaining pressure on Rabaul where airfields were receiving inflows of IJNAF reinforcements. Rabaul was hit on six nights, almost always in bad weather, with relatively large forces of a dozen or more 43rd and 90th Bomb Group aircraft per raid. Between July 1 and 3, 41 heavy bomber sorties were flown against Lakunai, Vunakanau, and Rapopo dropping almost 100 tons of bombs. Night fighters and antiaircraft fire harassed the raiders, but while several bombers were damaged, losses were only one 321st Squadron B-24D destroyed over Rabaul and one 63rd Squadron B-17F ditched off New Guinea with the crew being saved. No 9 Operational Group, meanwhile, kept up the pressure on the south coast of New Britain by launching the RAAF's largest raid of the campaign to that point. On July 22, ten No 100 Squadron Beauforts, six No 22 Squadron Bostons, and eight No 30 Squadron Beaufighters, accompanied by 38 Kittyhawks of Nos 75 and 77 Squadrons, pounded Gasmata by bombing and strafing the airstrip, antiaircraft positions, and the radio station. Only five Beaufighters were damaged by antiaircraft fire and no IJNAF fighters reacted.

Japanese attempts to hit back were ineffective, being severely limited by the need to fly airfield defense, convoy escort, and ground support missions, added to their mistaken focus on Kenney's diversionary airfield construction. A high rate of debilitating illness among recently arrived personnel also reduced sortie rates. Overall, Teramoto's aircraft

Shadows of three 19th Bomb Squadron "Silver Fleet" B-26s [one shown, inset] pass over camouflaged Japanese supply barges in New Britain's Borgen Bay at 1,000ft as a bomb falls toward them (upper left) on July 29, 1943. Such barges carried about 75 tons of supplies each that sustained Japanese forces and were thus prime Allied targets. (NARA/ Claringbould)

availability was often only about 25 percent, and only about 40 percent of its 1,308 sorties in July were offensive. However, on the morning of July 20, 24 24th Air Regiment Oscars and 30 68th and 78th Air Regiment Tonys escorted nine 208th Air Regiment Lilys to bomb targets in the New Guinea highlands. During the mission, five 68th Tonys came across a 320th Bomb Squadron B-24D conducting weather reconnaissance and shot it down at about 1020hrs, killing the crew. This was the first combat victory for the Tony in New Guinea. On the following day, 18 78th Tonys and 37 Oscars of the 24th and 59th Air Regiments engaged 26 P-38s of the 39th and 80th Fighter Squadrons. The Japanese fighters escorted eight Lilys that attacked targets near Salamaua while the P-38s had just finished escorting 405th Bomb Squadron B-25s bombing Bogadjim. The dogfight ranged from about 7,000ft to 18,000ft and resulted in two P-38s lost for two Tonys and two Oscars. On the 23rd, 28 39th and 80th P-38s again mixed it up with about two dozen 24th, 68th, and 78th Air Regiment fighters attacking 25 43rd Bomb Group B-17s and B-24s hitting Bogadjim. In the melee, one 80th P-38 was shot down with the pilot killed and one damaged 39th P-38 was later written off, while the Japanese losses included two Tonys and probably five Oscars. These and other dogfights during July took a significant toll on the Japanese fighter force. For example, by the end of July the 68th and 78th Air Regiments had only 23 serviceable Tonys between them, roughly a third of their assigned strength.

Gun camera still of a Tony in a head-on pass. After the Tony's theater debut in July 1943, it was frequently met in combat but never in large numbers as the 14th Air Brigade's 68th and 78th Air Regiments could not keep many serviceable. These units often pooled their Tonys to fly missions. (USAF)

Ramping up the pressure: Wewak and Balikpapan

Despite increased offensive action by SWPA units, claims of enemy aircraft downed over the course of June and July were less than a third of those claimed by SOPAC units in the Solomons. The Japanese were still in a relatively strong position. Kenney followed the IJAAF's build-up in the Wewak area via ULTRA intercepts and was worried that the Japanese would mount a massive strike against the Allies and upset the *Elkton III* timetable. This became even more concerning, since from June 1943 the JCS had been considering changing Pacific strategy simply to isolate rather than capture Rabaul. Such a major change would allow Nimitz to push forward more quickly with his Central Pacific offensive that would relegate the SWPA to a backwater unless MacArthur kept pace with westward progress in New Guinea. Therefore, MacArthur could brook no delays to *Elkton III*, and this meant Kenney had to redouble efforts to achieve Allied air supremacy. The key to keeping the Allied initiative was getting Tsili Tsili fully operational.

Meanwhile the Allies' air operations in early August prioritized the Lae–Salamaua area and secondarily targeted IJA supply operations along the New Guinea and New Britain coasts. Locating barge "hideouts," spaced 40–70 miles apart along the coasts, occupied at least 100 B-25 and A-20 sorties in the first half of August. Nos 22 and 30 Squadrons now at Vivigani, along with No 73 Wing's Kittyhawks, continued to be active in barge hunting along the New Britain coast. But the Allies directed their main effort against IJA positions opposite New Guinea Force. Antiaircraft batteries, storage facilities, supply nodes, and ammunition dumps were struck by at least 42 B-17, 154 B-24, 46 B-25, and nine B-26 sorties through August 17. The heaviest raid occurred on August 13 when the 43rd Bomb Group sortied 24 B-17s and B-24s, the 90th Bomb Group 23 B-24s, and the 22nd Bomb Group nine B-26s, together dropping 173 tons of bombs in the Salamaua area but with mixed results; many bombs missed and hit the Huon Gulf.

The Allies periodically attacked Salamaua from May to September 1943 to convince the Japanese 18th Army command to reinforce Salamaua by sending forces away from the Allies' intended assault objective: Lae. This 321st Bomb Squadron B-24D hits Salamaua from 5,400ft during a large-scale attack on August 13. (NARA)

Very poor weather in the first half of August limited Japanese operations. The only significant air combat occurred on August 2, when nine 24th Air Regiment Oscars escorted 18th Army commander Adachi flying from Madang in an 83rd Independent Squadron Sonia to inspect IJA positions around Salamaua. They unexpectedly ran into a 38th Bomb Group barge hunt east of Lae covered by 21 P-38s of the 9th and 80th Fighter Squadrons and lost at least two Oscars in a brief dogfight. Meanwhile, Adachi's plane prudently dove for the deck and diverted to Cape Gloucester. On August 12, 20 7th Air Regiment Helens and 22 14th Air Regiment Sallys bombed Mt. Hagen's grass airfield, and on the night of the 14th, seven Helens and seven Sallys bombed Wau. There was no Japanese air reaction to the major raid on Salamaua on August 13. In addition to the weather, this limited activity was probably due, at least in part, to some IJAAF disorganization, as 4th Air Army headquarters was just relocating to Wewak. Its presence there along with the headquarters of both 6th and 7th Air Divisions created friction among the staffs as lines of authority and operational procedures were ironed out. The Japanese were aware that their airfields were inadequate to maintain all the aircraft that had arrived or that were scheduled to arrive, and personnel were forced to engage in expanding airfield facilities without proper equipment. Disease was also taking its toll. Of 395 pilots assigned to 4th Air Army in August, 66 percent were incapacitated by malaria, dysentery, and other ailments. All this was a consequence of the IJA's lack of thorough preparation for air support in New Guinea, which would soon prove very costly.

Allied air activity in NEI complemented operations in eastern New Guinea. AVM Cole, who relieved Bladin as NWA commander in July, sent his forces to strike various air and maritime targets and also unveiled a major threat to the entire Japanese war effort. Just after midnight on August 13, 11 380th Bomb Group B-24Ds hit the Japanese oil refinery at Balikpapan on Borneo's east coast. Balikpapan supplied at least 35 percent of Japan's oil needs, including aviation fuel. Staging first to Darwin at midday on August 12 to top off wing fuel tanks and add bomb bay fuel tanks, the B-24Ds later took off at about 1700hrs on their roughly 2,700-mile round trip. The bombers caught their well-lit targets unawares and scored hits on the refinery, storage tanks, and the port. All but one B-24D returned to base after sunrise. The lone straggler dodged 202 Air Group Zeros over Timor and crash landed in a remote area of Western Australia damaged and low on fuel; the crew was picked up that same afternoon. The 380th flew a follow-up strike on the night of August 16–17 and nine bombed the harbor through heavy antiaircraft fire and reported sinking about 30,000 tons of shipping while losing no B-24Ds to antiaircraft or a recently transferred element of 202 Air Group Zeros. Thereafter, the 380th periodically struck other distant NEI strategic targets like Pomelaa, Soerabaja (Surabaya), and Tiepoe, in addition to the usual naval facilities and airfields, using a small RAAF airstrip at Corunna Downs in Western Australia to top off fuel before these longer missions.

The Allies intentionally left Wewak alone to lull 4th Air Army into a false sense of security, so that the Japanese would assume the Wewak complex lay beyond the reach of escorted daylight bombers. Meanwhile, Tsili Tsili construction was completed. On July 26, the first P-39s landed there, and the entire 40th and 41st Fighter Squadrons arrived by August 14. The 8th Fighter Squadron's new P-40Ns followed by August 30. Tsili Tsili boasted two runways and 75 dispersal hardstands, fuel and ammunition dumps, and a fighter control sector apparatus complete with communications and

Japanese maintenance personnel work on an Oscar in 1943. The extreme working conditions of frequent heavy rain, debilitating diseases, chronic lack of spare parts and maintenance equipment, and severe Allied air raids took an enormous toll on 4th Air Army's maintenance personnel and on its operational readiness. (AC)

The airfield at Tsili Tsili was vital in allowing fighters to support the Allied advance in the Huon Peninsula and escort bombers to Wewak. This early September 1943 view (looking east) shows three 35th Fighter Group P-39s (right) and two P-38s (upper center) in revetments, while on the left sit two C-47s and a B-17 transport. (NARA)

radar. The operational readiness of Tsili Tsili finally put Kenney in position to deliver a major blow to IJAAF power in SWPA, but the window for decisive action would not be open long. Because of its soil composition, Tsili Tsili would be practically useless once the rainy season began around September and October. Operation *Postern* was scheduled to begin September 4.

But Teramoto struck first. Having finally detected Tsili Tsili on August 14 with a midday Dinah reconnaissance flight, the next morning he mounted a raid on the airfield comprising seven 208th Air Regiment Lilys at 10,000ft protected by 12 Oscars of the 24th Air Regiment and 22 of the 59th Air Regiment. The 24th's fighters were at 15,000ft, while the 59th flew cover higher up. At about 0910hrs, the Japanese ran into two groups of 374th Troop Carrier Group C-47s, one heading for Tsili Tsili and the other for nearby Marilinan, escorted by a combined 27 35th Fighter Group P-39Ns. The fighters received orders to intercept the Japanese from the new Tsili Tsili controller, and in the ensuing melee the 59th Oscars shot down two C-47s near Tsili Tsili. The 24th Oscars, choosing to dogfight, left the Lilys unprotected and the 35th shot down six of them before bombing, along with three Oscars, while losing four P-39Ns with one pilot killed. Helens of the 7th Air Regiment attacked Tsili Tsili overnight, losing one to unknown causes, and the next day saw IJAAF fighters escort three Lilys to attack the airfield. At about 1430hrs on August 16, 16 340th Fighter Squadron P-47Ds orbiting Marilinan at about 11,000ft were bounced by 33 Oscars of the 24th and 59th Air Regiments sent to attack incoming transports. At around 1500hrs, the 431st Fighter Squadron, over Tsili Tsili at 18,000ft with 13 P-38s, also became embroiled in the fight. Each of the two new V Fighter Command groups claimed its first victories of the campaign. At least four Oscars were destroyed in exchange for two P-38s damaged and one P-47D shot down with the pilot lost. But the airfield was unscathed. About this time, 8th Area Army suspended plans to use 4th Air Army and 18th Army to capture Allied airfields in the New Guinea highlands, owing to an assessed inability to exploit any success. Consequently, the IJA 1st Raider paratroop unit intended for this operation was transferred to the NEI.

Kenney's turn came the next day. Shortly after midnight on August 17, the 43rd and 90th Bomb Groups put a total of 12 B-17E/Fs and 38 B-24Ds over the Wewak complex carrying fragmentation and incendiary cluster bomblets. The attack lasted over two hours and caused several fires and, more importantly, damaged communications lines. The 43rd

A gun camera frame of a 208th Air Regiment Lily caught in the sights of a 35th Fighter Squadron P-39N during the IJAAF assault on Tsili Tsili, August 15, 1943. The response of 4th Air Army to the expanding Allied air presence westward was generally spotty and ultimately ineffective. (USAF)

lost one B-24D that ditched west of Port Moresby with six crew rescued and the 90th lost two B-24Ds with their crews. Antiaircraft fire was reportedly heavy but inaccurate and two 13th Air Regiment Nicks got airborne from Boram and probably accounted for the 90th's losses. Following this attack, 5th Air Force launched 61 B-25Ds against the four-airfield complex later that same morning. Each carried a 300gal droppable auxiliary fuel tank in place of a belly turret, a recent modification, to enable them to make the roughly 1,000-mile round trip to Wewak. Only 32 aircraft actually attacked due to the 71st Bomb Squadron's 12 aircraft returning to Port Moresby after missing their rendezvous with escorting P-38s and nine 405th aircraft experiencing mechanical problems with their auxiliary fuel tanks, while the 3rd Bomb Group had nine aircraft abort for various mechanical reasons. The 8th Area Army had called for an inspection and awards ceremony to celebrate the reported, greatly inflated, results of the 4th Air Army's August 15 attack on Tsili Tsili and planned to dispatch a follow-up raid later that morning. Aircraft at Dagua and Boram were thus inadequately dispersed, and at Wewak they were lined up almost wingtip to wingtip on display. The Americans achieved complete surprise, since Teramoto did not believe the Allies were capable of such a strike, and in any event he did not receive any warning based on radar data usually transmitted from Rabaul, due to radar equipment malfunction. The Japanese also did not fix a communications outage with their spotters east of Wewak, caused by the overnight raid, until the B-25s were about to strike. Dagua, Wewak, and Boram were all bombed and strafed around 0950hrs, while But went undamaged since it had been the absent 71st Squadron's target. One 90th Squadron B-25D was shot down and one damaged by antiaircraft fire as they attacked a transport off Boram after hitting Wewak, and one 405th Squadron plane was damaged by 59th Air Regiment Oscars that chased it as it pulled away from its attack on Dagua. Against this, the 6th and 7th Air Divisions reported to higher headquarters only 28 and 12 aircraft left operational, respectively, out of more than 230 available the previous day.

Beginning at about 0900hrs the next morning, 5th Air Force attacked the Wewak complex again, but this time the Japanese were ready. Heavy bombers attacked, this time in daylight, though bad weather and mechanical troubles prevented 23 of 49 bombers from even reaching the target. Those that did from the 43rd and 90th Bomb Groups found very poor visibility and either dropped their bombs through the rain squalls with unobserved results or over water. Some ran into 24th Air Regiment Oscars near Hansa Bay, but they only suffered

The 59th Air Regiment arrived in New Guinea from the NEI in mid-July 1943. It was heavily involved in 4th Air Army operations between August 1943 and February 17, 1944, when it returned to Japan. Here, a 59th Oscar taxis at But, November 1943. (AC)

minor damage. The B-25s did better. Through heavy antiaircraft fire, the 3rd Bomb Group put 30 planes over Wewak and Boram, attacking the former's harbor and claiming a 1,000-ton transport sunk and hitting 12 aircraft and a fuel dump at the latter airfield. The 38th Bomb Group's 28 B-25s took on But and Dagua. The 71st Squadron made up for missing the previous day's attack by strafing and dropping 360 parafrag and 129 daisy cutter clusters on But, while the 405th Squadron attacked Dagua with strafing and 36 parafrag clusters. Some B-25s were forced to divert to Muschu Island just off the coast where they strafed a dozen barges off its west shore and dropped 43 parafrag clusters indiscriminately over the island. The B-25s were disrupted by effective antiaircraft fire and fighters that engaged them before, during, and after their attack runs. At least 16 24th and 59th Air Regiment Oscars, five 68th Tonys, and two 13th Nicks tangled with both B-25 groups and with some of the 74 475th Fighter Group P-38s that entered the low-altitude fight from about 4,500ft once they spotted the Japanese through the clouds. The running battle resulted in at least 25 Japanese fighters shot down, according to 4th Air Army reports. The Japanese shot down one 38th B-25D, one 3rd B-25D, and one 475th P-38, with all aircrew lost, and one 38th B-25D was written off after crash landing at Seven-Mile 'Drome.

The destruction wrought over these two days was monumental. Though the exact number of IJAAF aircraft destroyed will never be known, the two-day total probably falls between Japanese records indicating about 37 destroyed and damaged on the ground, and MacArthur's GHQ communique claiming 187. Regardless, 4th Air Army was practically wiped out and required a major infusion of aircraft to carry on the fight. However, there was no let-up as the 5th restruck Wewak's airfields on August 20 (Boram), August 21 (But and Dagua), August 24 (Wewak), August 29 (Wewak and Boram), and August 30 (But and Dagua) to ensure they remained suppressed ahead of *Postern*. The official USAAF assessment for all Japanese aircraft destroyed in SWPA on the ground during August was 175, so in mounting this series of raids Kenney guaranteed MacArthur's *Elkton III* timetable would not be upset by enemy air attack. The cost to 5th Air Force was low – three B-24s, two B-25s and six P-38s.

Divide and conquer – Huon Peninsula and Western New Britain

The August obliteration of 4th Air Army at Wewak was accompanied by strikes on other targets supporting IJA resistance on the Huon Peninsula. Supply shipping and storage sites received much attention. The 89th Bomb Squadron's A-20Gs and No 9 Operational Group's bombers kept up the pressure on New Guinea and New Britain barge traffic, while 5th Air Force paid particular attention to the area between Hansa Bay and Bogadjim. A major raid on August 25 against shipping and facilities at Nubia and Awar, on Hansa Bay, saw the 38th Bomb Group strike several barges, a large transport, and bivouac areas at Nubia while the 3rd Bomb Group hit Awar. Immediately after, the 43rd and 90th Bomb Groups dropped 1,000lb and 500lb bombs on Nubia and Awar, respectively. Antiaircraft fire was light and Japanese fighters absent. The Japanese reported four ships sunk, four damaged, 72 killed and 120 wounded, and three houses, three searchlights, and 4,800 artillery rounds destroyed. The 3rd Bomb Group sent 26 B-25s on another attack on a Wewak resupply flotilla on August 28, claiming 16 supply craft destroyed while losing one B-25 to the explosion of another aircraft's bomb.

On September 1 the 5th dropped its largest tonnage of bombs to date when 24 38th Bomb Group B-25s and 13 43rd and 18 90th Bomb Group B-24s hit Alexishafen, while 20 90th Bomb Group B-24s hit Madang, with a total of 201 tons of bombs. New Britain also came in for attention. Cape Gloucester was struck on August 30 by nine 19th Bomb Squadron B-26s, undamaged by heavy antiaircraft fire, and on September 2 by nine B-26s and 13 43rd Bomb Group B-17s and B-24s. During this latter mission, the B-26s reported good bombing results but antiaircraft fire damaged four bombers. For the heavies attacking 30 minutes later thunderheads developed over the target and allowed only six to drop their bombs from 9,000ft. One B-17E was lost to a 13th Air Regiment Nick. September 3 saw daytime raids by heavies on Cape Gloucester, on Lae gun emplacements by 12 Beaufighters, 18 B-25s, and nine B-26s, and nighttime bombing of Rabaul airfields by 11 Cairns-based Nos 11 and 20 Squadron Catalinas, shifted from NEI minelaying operations for this mission. *Postern* was scheduled to begin the next morning.

During a major operation against Hansa Bay-area targets on August 25, 1943, 43rd Bomb Group B-24s dropped 87 1,000lb antipersonnel bombs on Nubia airfield, some shown here just after bursting as seen from a 71st Bomb Squadron B-25. These bombs detonated above ground spreading shrapnel to hit personnel taking shelter in foxholes and slit trenches. (NARA)

The IJAAF used Nicks mainly to combat US heavy bombers. This 13th Air Regiment Nick, while transiting from Rabaul to Boram, force-landed at Cape Gloucester on September 2, 1943. A 9th Fighter Squadron P-38H damaged it after it attacked 65th Bomb Squadron B-17s targeting Cape Gloucester airfield. (NARA)

The Allies made special arrangements for air cover of the Australian 9th Division's amphibious landing near Hopoi, roughly 15–20 miles east of Lae. The debate over fighters providing air cover versus being on ground alert that had arisen for *Chronicle* was resolved for *Postern* by MacArthur. The RAAF would escort the amphibious task force from Milne Bay to its pre-assault staging area at Buna, and 5th Air Force would provide 32 fighters over Barbey's VII Amphib during daylight on D-day while other squadrons maintained ground alert. Also, the coverage of the air warning system in place, consisting of radar sites at Bena Bena, Tsili Tsili, Bulolo, Morobe, Cape Ward Hunt, and Dobodura and fighter control sectors at Tsili Tsili, Dobodura, and Vivigani, was deemed inadequate owing to limited equipment range and potential terrain masking. So, at the suggestion of a No 9 Operational Group staff officer, the USN destroyer *Reid* was positioned about 45nm southeast of Finschhafen to add its radar to the warning network and provide fighter control services.

On September 4, the first 9th Division troops landed at about 0630hrs. Using cloud cover, the IJAAF attacked the invasion force at about 0730hrs with three Lilys and six Oscars staging from Lae. They seriously damaged two landing craft infantry (LCI) before fighter cover of 16 40th and 41st Fighter Squadron P-39Ns and 14 433rd P-38s could intervene, but a 475th HQ P-38 claimed one IJNAF Zero destroyed, possibly on reconnaissance, while a P-38 was lost with its pilot to unknown causes. A more serious threat from the IJNAF developed in the early afternoon. Twelve 751 Air Group Bettys armed with torpedoes, eight 582 Air Group Vals, and 61 Zeros arrived from Rabaul at about 1320hrs and headed toward Morobe where they found the second echelon of the invasion force. There were seven USAAF fighter squadrons in the Lae–Salamaua area and elements of four engaged IJNAF aircraft between about 1330hrs and 1430hrs. Pilots of the 39th, 80th, 342nd and 433rd Squadrons claimed 15 Zeros, a Val and four Bettys shot down, though the IJNAF reported only four Zeros and three Bettys downed, with another Betty and two Vals crash-landing at Rabaul. Japanese attacks put two fully loaded landing ships tank (LST) and two LCIs out of action and damaged two destroyers. That night and for several nights thereafter, single Japanese aircraft overflew the invasion beaches, Morobe, Buna, and Oro Bay, reconnoitering Allied shipping and dropping a few bombs, causing very little trouble beyond keeping personnel awake.

The Allies executed the second part of *Postern* the next morning, a well-coordinated operation at Nadzab, about 18 miles northwest of Lae. After a six-squadron B-25 parafrag and strafing run at 0944hrs, at 1012hrs three pairs of 89th Bomb Group A-20Gs flew at very low altitude laying long lines of smoke to obscure the drop zone from any IJA troops. They were followed by 81 C-47s at 1022hrs dropping 1,700 paratroopers of the US 503rd

Parachute Infantry Regiment and part of the 2/4 Field Regiment of the Australian 7th Division on the Nadzab clearing. The drop, covered by 100 fighters, took less than five minutes and was observed by a "brass hats flight" (Kenney's term) of three 43rd Bomb Group B-17s, two carrying MacArthur and Kenney in separate aircraft, and an escort flying near the drop zone. The rapid operation was unopposed both in the air and on the ground. The Allies immediately began to prepare the area and within nine days Nadzab had two 6,000ft runways and dispersal space to handle 36 C-47s. The Second Air Task Force moved to Nadzab from Tsili Tsili. The remainder of the 7th Division was flown in and by September 10 had begun moving toward Lae from the west to capture it in a pincer movement in conjunction with the 9th Division pushing from the east. Lae was captured on September 16. During this period, 5th Air Force bombers flew 421 sorties against Lae-area targets.

During September, the Allies and Japanese both received reinforcements. Kenney's 54th Troop Carrier Wing added the 433rd Troop Carrier Group and the remainder of the 317th Troop Carrier Group, giving it 17 squadrons. The full 345th Bomb Group returned to action September 5 after its B-25Ds were converted to strafers in Australia. The RAAF added No 24 Squadron, equipped with Vultee Vengeance dive bombers, at Kenney's specific request. This squadron arrived at Tsili Tsili with 17 aircraft on September 2, soon moving to Dobodura, and went into action around Lae from September 7. Nos 6 and 8 Squadrons, reequipped with Beauforts, both resumed operations at Milne Bay and Vivigani, respectively. In Brisbane, Fleet Air Wing 17 (FAW-17) began operations on September 15 with USN PBY-5A Catalina patrol squadrons VP-11, 52 and 101 assigned. These American PBY-5As, like their RAAF counterparts, conducted reconnaissance, anti-shipping (Black Cat) and air-sea rescue (Dumbo) missions during the campaign. On attack missions they normally carried either four 500lb bombs or a torpedo and two bombs. They operated from Port Moresby and with the seaplane tenders *San Pablo* and *Half Moon* at Samarai, near Milne Bay, and came under No 9 Operational Group for tasking. On the night of September 16,

Eighty-one 374th Troop Carrier Group C-47s drop the 503rd Parachute Infantry Regiment at Nadzab at 1022hrs on September 5, 1943. The drop lasted only four and a half minutes. Six 89th Bomb Squadron A-20Gs laid the smoke in the background just before the drop began, to conceal the paratroops from potential Japanese ground fire. (NARA)

a VP-11 aircraft got that unit's first SWPA kill against a transport it bombed and strafed off Wewak. USN Black Cats flew almost every night around New Guinea, New Britain, and New Ireland regardless of the weather, and GHQ communiques often mentioned they were the only aircraft on operations on a given day.

For its part, the IJAAF filtered into New Guinea more than 200 additional aircraft, a mix of fighters and bombers. This activity, monitored by the RAAF No 3 Wireless Unit at Darwin, was a recurring pattern until early April 1944, with anywhere from a few to three dozen aircraft arriving in each of several shipments per month. In almost all cases pilots of units already stationed in New Guinea that had lost most or all of their aircraft were transported to Manila to ferry the new aircraft to their bases. The only newly arriving unit was the 61st Air Regiment, whose Helens were assigned to But to operate with the 7th Air Regiment. Once replenished, the IJAAF raided Nadzab on the afternoon of September 20 with nine 14th Air Regiment Sallys and ten probable 68th Air Regiment Tonys. The raid killed two men working on the airfield and shot down one 432nd Fighter Squadron P-38 with the pilot lost; the 432nd claimed two Tonys. That night the IJAAF conducted its last raid of the New Guinea campaign against Port Moresby using just two Helens. The next day another IJAAF raid in the Lae area at dusk was broken up by 8th Fighter Squadron P-40Ns. They first chased a 10th Air Regiment Dinah on reconnaissance then tangled with Oscars and about nine possible Helens, claiming four Oscars and two bombers for one P-40N shot down by bomber return fire from a tail gun with the pilot saved.

In September the Allies continued to focus on the Huon Gulf while building up Nadzab into their major airbase in New Guinea. Base expansion was critical to allow both bombers and fighters to start closer to Japanese strongpoints further west. The Allies began additional airfields as New Guinea Force troops captured suitable locations in the

The 4th Air Army received a continuous stream of replacement aircraft for combat and operational (accidental) losses between mid-1943 and April 1944. The route usually flown was Japan–Formosa–Philippines–NEI–New Guinea. Here, replacement Helens, already camouflaged, head for New Guinea probably in late 1943 to be assigned to the 7th Air Regiment. (AC)

Ramu River valley by late September, with Gusap being the primary project. Meanwhile, the Allies continued to pound IJA troops and their supply lines, both on land and at sea. Time was critical; the CCS had formally decided at the Quadrant conference in late August that Rabaul would not be seized, merely isolated. Thus, MacArthur moved up the timetable for taking Finschhafen on the east coast of the Huon Peninsula. Finschhafen had another key airfield the Allies needed as well as good naval facilities. Allied air power targeted IJA positions in the area heavily, led by the RAAF employing No 4 Squadron's Wirraways and Boomerangs and No 24 Squadron's Vengeances against point targets such as gun emplacements and command posts. The 5th usually employed the 89th and 19th Bomb Squadrons in "softening up" Finschhafen. The unfinished overland supply route the Japanese were building from Madang to the peninsula was attacked at various points from Bogadjim eastward, with B-17s, B-24s, B-25s, and the 35th Fighter Group's two P-39 squadrons. Maritime supply movements and airfields around New Britain were kept under assault, especially by the RAAF, during which No 9 Operational Group lost 12 bombers and ten aircrews to antiaircraft fire.

The NWA was also busy in September to draw Japanese units away from the Allies' Huon Peninsula operations. RAAF Catalinas flying out of Darwin conducted nocturnal minelaying at several Japanese-held ports, from Sorong to Soerabaja. While Nos 18 and 31 Squadrons concentrated on airfields and other facilities on Timor, Ambon, and Ceram, the 380th Bomb Group added Makassar and Kendari to its target list. Typical of the 380th's missions was a daylight raid flown on September 21. Nine 380th Bomb Group B-24Ds hit the IJNAF's Langgoer (Langgur) airfield. About 25 IJNAF and IJAAF fighters intercepted and a 5th Air Regiment Nick seriously damaged one B-24D that crash landed on an offshore reef; some of the crew drowned but others were captured by a Japanese patrol boat. The 380th also bombed Manokwari and Sorong, the latter being struck three times.

At 0445hrs on September 22, Barbey's VII Amphib began landing 5,300 Australian 20th Brigade troops at a beach seven miles north of Finschhafen. The landing was not covered by Allied fighters but initially met with no Japanese air opposition. The *Reid* once

A No 20 Squadron "Black Cat" Catalina pictured in January 1944. Used by both the RAAF and the USN, Black Cats conducted primarily nighttime anti-shipping operations. The RAAF Catalina and USN PBY-5A squadrons conducted reconnaissance, night bombing attacks and port mining in supporting the Cape Gloucester and Hollandia operations. (AWM)

again performed radar picket duties but this time it was closer to shore. A flight of 751 Air Group Bettys returning to Rabaul from a dawn raid near Nadzab spotted the landing force approaching the beach and alerted 11th Air Fleet, and there were probably IJAAF reconnaissance planes in the area as early as 0945hrs. Between about 1130hrs and 1300hrs IJNAF aircraft and what may have been an IJAAF strafing group arrived over the landing area. Eight 751 Air Group Bettys armed with torpedoes flew in at about 1245hrs at very low altitude, covered by 38 Zeros of the 201, 204 and 253 Air Groups. The Japanese claimed several vessels sunk, but all torpedoes missed. By chance, the American fighter cover was due to turn over just as the strike arrived, placing multiple squadrons in the area. Directed by *Reid*, elements of the loitering 35th, 39th, 80th and 341st Fighter Squadrons along with arriving 9th and 432nd Squadrons broke up the main attack, while a 342nd Squadron P-47D shot down a possible IJNAF Dinah reconnaissance plane. The duel in and out of clouds resulted in total claims of 40 Japanese aircraft destroyed for three P-38s and two pilots lost, while the amphibious vessels escaped damage. The 9th Squadron reported combat with a few IJAAF aircraft over the beach and claimed three, but no IJAAF losses were reported that day. The IJNAF reported losing six Bettys and eight Zeros, most from 201 Air Group, with at least two Betty crewmen captured by *Reid*. The IJNAF targeted the Finschhafen area again on September 24 with nine Bettys that destroyed the Allied air liaison command post at the newly captured airfield, and small nighttime Japanese harassment raids continued intermittently until at least October 17. But these limited attacks could not thwart the Australian 9th Division, supported by Allied air support, from slowly pushing the IJA out of the Huon Peninsula. The 9th Division later moved along the coast and linked up with the 7th Division fighting from Nadzab up the Markham and Ramu Valleys toward Bogadjim. Support for New Guinea Force included A-20Gs, Vengeances, Wirraways, and Boomerangs blasting IJA Huon Peninsula positions, and almost daily B-25 barge hunting sweeps along the coasts of New Britain and New Guinea up to Madang.

The 4th Air Army reached a low ebb in terms of operational aircraft about the time of the Finschhafen assault. It continued to receive replacement aircraft but experienced a combat capability shortfall as veteran fighter units left. The 24th Air Regiment transferred back to Japan on October 2, leaving its Oscars to the 13th and 68th Air Regiments, both of which were short of Nicks and Tonys, respectively. The 59th Air Regiment was also inactive for the month in the Philippines, only returning on October 31. Its 15 Oscars were also distributed to the two Tony units, the 68th and 78th Air Regiments. A new Oscar unit, the 248th Air Regiment, arrived with 30 Oscars at Alexishafen by October 30, but for most of that month 4th

A No 4 Squadron Wirraway crew studies maps with Australian 9th Division liaison officers at Finschhafen before a ground support mission, October 30, 1943. No 4 provided close support during the Huon Peninsula and Markham/Ramu Valley fighting. The squadron also guided other Allied attack aircraft to targets in the featureless jungle terrain. (AWM)

No 24 Squadron Hits Yamada Force

The Allied decision to assault Finschhafen was made on September 17, with the attack scheduled for the 22nd. The defending IJA troops of Lieutenant General Yamada were dug in around Finschhafen and at Sattelberg, a 3,240ft peak that commanded a view of the proposed landing area and of Finschhafen to the south. To prepare the area for the landing Allied aircraft flew several raids in the area. On the morning of September 18, 14 No 24 Squadron Vultee Vengeances flying from Tsili Tsili attacked several targets around Finschhafen, including huts and some identified gun emplacements in the rough terrain. The Vengeances first dropped 500lb demolition bombs, diving to 1,400ft for their release to ensure an accurate stike. They then strafed identified positions and returned without damage. The mode of attack was a bit more daring than the prescribed Vengeance release altitude of about 3,500ft.

Jim Laurier

The 348th Fighter Group first saw combat on August 16 near Tsili Tsili and participated in many air battles thereafter. Here, a ground crewman guides a 341st Fighter Squadron P-47D taxiing through the dust at Finschhafen in December 1943. Its theater-developed 200gal "Brisbane" belly drop tank provided the range to reach combat areas, but it imposed significant aerodynamic limitations. (USMC)

Air Army was shorthanded of battle-tested fighter pilots. Added to this were the ongoing maintenance problems due to lack of trained personnel, parts, and equipment. The 26th Air Regiment, flying Sonias, arrived at But on October 23 and soon sent detachments forward to Alexishafen and Cape Gloucester to conduct reconnaissance and nighttime harassment bombing on the Huon Peninsula and in the Vitiaz Strait. The 7th and 61st Air Regiments' Helens mostly flew night harassment or transport missions.

The 5th Air Force reattacked Wewak-area targets during the last half of September to address the influx of new IJAAF aircraft. Several air battles developed during these attacks as 4th Air Army tried to protect its major bases, but its losses in the air and on the ground ran to more than 60 over this period. And with the move forward of the Allied "fighter line," using recently operational airstrips such as Lae, Marilinan, Tsili Tsili, Nadzab, and others for staging or recovery, ADVON could now send even P-47Ds and P-40Ns on fighter sweeps westward, activity previously only available to P-38 units. One such mission on October 11 saw four 348th Fighter Group P-47Ds clash with around three dozen Oscars and Tonys near Boram, claiming nine for no loss. These sweeps contributed to establishing Allied air supremacy in the coming months.

During October, 5th Air Force added a new anti-shipping weapon. Thirteen XB-24 (also referred to as SB-24) "Snoopers" joined the 63rd Bomb Squadron. Also known as the "Scott Project" after the unit's commander during stateside work-ups, these aircraft and their crews were specially equipped and trained for nighttime, low-altitude attacks on Japanese shipping and for pathfinder missions. A 63rd Snooper flew its first mission the night of October 21–22 and made three unsuccessful runs, two level from 1,500ft and one skip-bomb from a couple hundred feet that were all near misses on a large transport. Also, the 75mm cannon-armed B-25Gs of the 38th Bomb Group's 822nd and 823rd Squadrons arrived at Dobodura on October 9–10, ready for operations. However, Kenney did not receive all the P-38s he had been promised. Only 45 arrived between October and December, reducing his inventory from 212 in September to only 150 by February 1944. He did receive 207 more P-47Ds, which he used not only for the 348th Fighter Group but also to re-equip the whole 35th Fighter Group and the 9th and 36th Fighter Squadrons in November. The 9th and 39th Fighter Squadrons' P-38s went to the 475th Fighter Group.

Rabaul interlude

For the next phase of *Elkton III*, and to support planned SOPAC operations against Bougainville, Rabaul again moved to the top of Kenney's target list. Photographic and ULTRA intelligence revealed the recent arrival of additional IJNAF aircraft. At least 128 bombers, 145 fighters, and 30 reconnaissance/transport aircraft were at Rabaul by October 11. Kenney planned a series of large daylight raids to treat Rabaul as he had Wewak. Staging six P-38 escort squadrons from the two RAAF airstrips on Kiriwina made the daylight missions feasible.

The first blow in SWPA's Rabaul "campaign" was an October 12 attack led by 107 B-25s and 12 Beaufighters to suppress Vunakanau and Rapopo airfields followed by 87 B-24s to hit Simpson Harbor shipping. Cover was provided by 101 P-38s. The 90th Bomb Group battled through heavy antiaircraft fire and about three dozen intercepting Zeros that pursued some B-24s about 175 miles from Rabaul. The Zeros were themselves attacked by the 475th Fighter Group and 80th Fighter Squadron, which together claimed three. Two 90th B-24s, one 405th Bomb Squadron B-25, and one Beaufighter were lost with crews, and a 403rd Bomb Squadron B-24D ditched just off Kiriwina with antiaircraft damage. After the mission Kenney claimed three large transports, 43 smaller transports, and 73 small harbor craft, but Japanese records stated only the 5,800-ton *Keisho Maru* and two luggers were sunk and three destroyers damaged. The 11th Air Flotilla admitted two Zeros lost, nine aircraft destroyed and 36 damaged on the ground, and 4th Air Army lost six destroyed and eight damaged. Bad weather precluded another try at Rabaul until October 18.

During October, a back-and-forth slugfest between the IJNAF and Allies ensued. Bettys conducted attacks, mostly at night, on 13 days between October 8 and 25 against the Huon Peninsula, Morobe, Buna/Oro Bay, and Goodenough Island but caused little damage. The IJNAF mounted a daylight raid on Oro Bay on October 15, which the Japanese command knew was a main staging point for Allied amphibious assaults. However, the 15 582 Air Group Vals and 39 204 Air Group Zeros that engaged in the morning attack met with stiff resistance from the 49th and 475th Fighter Groups. One 431st Fighter Squadron P-38 was shot down with the pilot saved, while the Japanese lost 14 Vals and five Zeros and did almost no damage to their shipping targets. Since the weather still disallowed a Rabaul strike, 5th Air Force returned to Wewak the next day when 36 345th Bomb Group B-25Ds hit several aircraft and antiaircraft positions at Boram and Wewak with 100lb daisy cutter bombs and by strafing at around 1040hrs. Fifteen 80th Fighter Squadron P-38s claimed five fighters destroyed, probably from the 78th Air Regiment.

The first major SWPA daylight raid on Rabaul-area targets on October 12, 1943, caught many IJNAF and IJAAF aircraft on the ground. Here, three 702 Air Group Bettys are under attack at Vunakanau as parademos drift down on their revetments and explosions begin (upper right). (NARA)

The Wewak area was periodically attacked as Allied intelligence revealed influxes of aircraft to replenish IJAAF losses. Above, two 405th Bomb Squadron B-25Ds pass a smoking Dagua airfield just after their attack on October 22, 1943; below, a 7th Air Regiment Helen being readied at Dagua that day for a mission is damaged during the Allied attack. (NARA)

On October 17, the IJAAF sent six probable 208th Air Regiment Lilys escorted by about a dozen Oscars and Tonys to hit Finschhafen while the IJNAF made another apparent attempt against Morobe and Oro Bays that fared just as badly as before. Four 41st Fighter Squadron P-39Ns tangled with the IJAAF aircraft at 12,000ft at about 1030hrs and claimed five Lilys and an Oscar for one P-39N shot down with the pilot saved. The Lilys turned away without dropping their bombs. Around the same time, about 30 11th Air Fleet Zeros, with probably some IJAAF Rabaul-based 68th Air Regiment Tonys thrown in, were intercepted by the 475th and 49th Fighter Groups north of the coast. In a dogfight between 20,000ft and the water, the American fighters claimed 13, at least one of which was probably a Tony, for the loss of one 433rd P-38 and one 7th P-40N with pilots. That night, six Bettys attacked Finschhafen and reported one unidentified explosion. On October 22, the 38th Bomb Group sent 24 71st and 405th Bomb Squadron B-25Ds, escorted by the 348th's P-47Ds, to strike But and Dagua, while five 822nd B-25Gs bombed and strafed shipping around Kairiru and Muschu Islands. No IJAAF fighters reacted and antiaircraft was light and inaccurate, and the 822nd's 75mm cannons proved effective against the barges.

Weather seemed to improve enough for another shot at Rabaul on October 18, but storms closed in quickly over New Britain after the raid was launched. However, 54 B-25s, ignoring a weather-related recall order, were able to get through under the rainstorms to hit Tobera and Rapopo, while the P-38 escort and the B-24s, including some 380th Bomb Group aircraft temporarily shifted from NWA, flying at higher altitudes aborted. The B-25s of the 38th and 345th Bomb Groups claimed significant destruction of 39 aircraft on the ground along with the 5,000-ton freighter *Kinkasan Maru* and a corvette while losing only three B-25s to about 60 intercepting Zeros. Aircrews reported fewer Japanese aircraft on the ground than on the previous raid, possibly because the Japanese moved at least some aircraft to Kavieng, which they sometimes used as a dispersal airfield.

Between October 23 and 25, the weather improved sufficiently for a series of strikes on Rabaul. While the 201, 204, and 253 Air Groups sortied large numbers of Zeros in defense, they reportedly were not aggressive and only downed two P-38s, one B-25, and one B-24 over this period. The 5th made exaggerated claims of 86 aircraft destroyed on the ground and 100 in the air, although the Japanese admitted the attack greatly disrupted operations. Also, starting on October 25, RAAF Command sent Catalinas of all three squadrons from Cairns against Kavieng every night for a week. The 29th saw 37 B-24s attack Vunakanau, dropping a mix of 100lb fragmentation and 500lb demolition bombs. The bombers were covered by 53 P-38s and the mission claimed 45 Japanese aircraft on the ground and 18 in the air for no losses, although many bombers were damaged. No 8 Squadron Beauforts flew that night against Tobera airfield and hit the dispersal area and supply dumps east of the airfield.

A large number of IJNAF aircraft arrived at Rabaul's airfields from the large IJN base at Truk by November 1. These included 66 Zeros from the 1st Carrier Division's *Zuikaku*, *Shokaku*, and *Zuiho* air groups along with dive and torpedo bombers. With this massive reinforcement, the Japanese conducted strikes against the SOPAC amphibious assault against Empress Augusta Bay at Bougainville, which occurred the morning of November 1. With favorable weather reported over Rabaul by 8th Photo Reconnaissance Squadron F-5s, 5th Air Force mounted another large Rabaul raid on November 2 in support of SOPAC, unaware of the presence of so many additional IJNAF fighters. Even so, total IJNAF operational strength was about 200 aircraft, only a third of the aircraft present at Rabaul. That morning 76 B-25s met 80 P-38 escorts over Oro Bay, headed for New Britain, and then followed the coast at about 1,000ft to circle past the peaks northeast of the harbor to hit Rabaul from the north. The defenders were alerted to an attack by a New Ireland lookout and two patrolling destroyers off Cape Gazelle. First, the 39th and 80th Fighter Squadrons swept over Simpson Harbor to draw off any Zeros. Between 60 and 150 Zeros dove on the P-38s from 6,000ft and a massive dogfight erupted over the harbor. The first wave of B-25s comprised the 345th Bomb Group squadrons, which dropped parafrags and 100lb white phosphorous bombs, so-called "Kenney Cocktails," over Rabaul town, docks, antiaircraft sites, and Lakunai airfield, and then strafed. They were followed by 3rd and 38th Bomb Group B-25s attacking harbor shipping. When the attack concluded, 5th Air Force claimed 16 aircraft destroyed on the ground, 68 in the air, and ten seaplanes in the harbor, along with 50,000 tons of shipping. Actual Japanese losses totaled 20 aircraft and between 5,000 and 13,000 tons of shipping sunk with 22 other vessels damaged. Nine P-38s and eight B-25s were lost with 45 aircrew. Kenney and many of his aircrew considered this their toughest fight of the campaign.

Both the IJNAF and IJAAF occasionally employed air-to-air phosphorous bombs throughout the campaign but they achieved little success. During the November 2 Rabaul raid, some 253 Air Group Zeros dropped IJNAF Type 99 No 3 33.7kg *Ta-dan* bombs to counter attacking 345th Bomb Group B-25s. A targeted B-25 appears at extreme left. (NARA)

The 38th Bomb Group came in behind the 345th and endured attacks by antiaircraft and fighters. One of the eight participating 71st Bomb Squadron B-25D-1s overflies the probable 1,550-ton *Haruna Maru* in Simpson Harbor at about 1345hrs during the Rabaul attack on November 2, 1943. Rabaul's dock area burns in the background. (NARA)

A Beaufort crew flies in a multi-squadron formation en route to Lindenhafen, January 17, 1944. Beaufort squadrons persistently conducted bombing and torpedo attacks from Milne Bay, Vivigani, and Kiriwina against New Britain targets, including night raids on Rabaul. Nos 8 and 100 Squadrons moved west with No 10 Operational Group in early May 1944. (AWM)

The next move against Rabaul was on the afternoon of November 5, when the 5th followed a crippling morning raid by SOPAC on an IJN cruiser force in Simpson Harbor by bombing the Rabaul dock area with 27 B-24s with a P-38 escort. For the week, 5th Air Force and SOPAC attacks accounted for 83 IJNAF aircraft, 44 of them from Kusaka's 11th Air Fleet. The 43rd Bomb Group made the 5th's last attacks against Rabaul on November 10 and 11. First, the 403rd Bomb Squadron dropped fragmentation bomb clusters on Lakunai just before dawn on the 10th. The next day the 64th again hit Lakunai before dawn with 100lb demolition bombs and fragmentation clusters. Searchlights and heavy antiaircraft fire met both missions, but only one 403rd B-24 was lost, probably to antiaircraft fire.

RAAF units were also active during this period. On the night of November 2–3, between 2200hrs and 0300hrs, 16 Beauforts of Nos 6, 8, and 100 Squadrons sortied from Vivigani and Kiriwina to strike Tobera. One Beaufort was driven off before bombing by a 251 Air Group Irving. On the night of November 5, three No 8 Squadron Beauforts used torpedoes against shipping in Keravia Bay, while four No 100 Squadron Beauforts bombed nearby Vunakanau airfield, but results were unobserved. Beauforts hit Rabaul targets with torpedoes and bombs on November 8, 10, 14, and 17, claiming hits on various ships but without confirmed results, while losing two Beauforts and crews. Over the next month, RAAF Beauforts continued nighttime strikes on Rabaul and New Ireland targets in conjunction with SOPAC to limit any IJNAF response to the upcoming *Elkton III* New Britain operations.

Another RAAF development was the stand-up of No 10 Operational Group at Nadzab on November 13. Kenney requested this in September with the idea that No 10 would be a "mobile" force, initially subordinate to No 9 Operational Group, that could occupy newly won airfields quickly and thus be capable of supporting the rapid westward movements MacArthur envisioned. The new group was commanded by Gp Capt. Scherger. It was composed of two wings, No 77 with attack squadrons and No 78 with fighter squadrons. This came to fruition in January when Nos 75 and 78 Squadrons' Kittyhawks arrived, joining No 4 Squadron's Wirraways and Boomerangs and No 24 Squadron's Vengeances. The group was later augmented by Nos 21, 23 (Vengeance), and 80 (Kittyhawk) Squadrons and was primarily focused on assisting the Allied troops pushing along the coast and through the Ramu Valley toward Bogadjim and Madang.

Corking the Rabaul bottle – Cape Gloucester, Saidor, Kavieng, and the Admiralties

Over the rest of November and the first half of December, the Allies prepared for the seizure of Cape Gloucester (Operation *Dexterity*). For the air forces, this required directly supporting New Guinea Force units fighting on the Huon Peninsula and in the Ramu Valley to keep the IJA on the defensive. It also required fully developing forward airfields needed to support MacArthur's upcoming offensive, which for various reasons could not be done until about December 15. These included Gusap, site of the Third Air Task Force, Finschhafen, and Nadzab. The maintenance of pressure on enemy airstrips that could facilitate counterattacks against the upcoming amphibious landings was also required. Accordingly, along with Rabaul, Cape Gloucester, Gasmata, Talasea, and Cape Hoskins on New Britain were subjected to repeated strikes. On New Guinea, Alexishafen and Madang were the prime targets, with coastal supply nodes also getting attention. ADVON also relied heavily on No 9 Operational Group during this period, not only for New Britain barge hunting by Beaufighters and

Bostons but also for Kittyhawks to escort 5th Air Force bombers and for independent attacks on Japanese airfields.

Additional 5th Air Force order-of-battle changes occurred around this time. In addition to the November swap-out of P-38s for P-47s, Kenney gained bomber and reconnaissance units. A light bomber unit, the 312th Bomb Group, arrived with P-40Ns with pilots trained in both dive- bombing and fighter interception. Its four squadrons were based at Gusap and began operations on December 14. Two squadrons of the 71st Reconnaissance Group began operations in November. The 82nd Reconnaissance Squadron (Fighter), flying P-39Qs, and the 17th Reconnaissance Squadron (Bomber), flying B-25Ds, operated from Dobodura by late November. An 82nd P-39Q claimed the group's first kill on December 18 over the Huon Peninsula, a probable 26th Air Regiment Sonia. A third unit, the 110th Reconnaissance Squadron (Fighter), flying P-39Ns, began operations on December 21 from Port Moresby before moving to Gusap. In mid-November, the 418th Night Fighter Squadron, using P-70s and a few P-38s, began operations from Dobodura attached to First Air Task Force. However, it was hampered by poorly trained radar operators using obsolescent SCR-270 and SCR-527 radars.

After a maintenance stand down to recover from the Rabaul effort, the 5th's B-24s slammed Alexishafen on November 13 and 15. Gasmata was hit by B-24s on November 20, 21, 22, 24, and 26, with B-25s joining in the November 22 attack, receiving a total of 440 tons of bombs from those raids. Cape Gloucester received B-24 visits on November 22 and 30 and saw B-25s and B-26s on November 29. On November 21, however, MacArthur decided to substitute Arawe for Gasmata as part of Operation *Dexterity*. Kenney could better support a landing there as it was 86 miles west of Gasmata, well within range of his fighters flying from Finschhafen and Nadzab. Therefore, the heavy attacks on Gasmata became diversionary to keep 8th Area Army guessing as to where an Allied assault on New Britain would happen. Wewak received further attention between November 27 and 28. B-25s from the 38th and 345th Bomb Groups hit Wewak and Boram airfields and transports near Cape Moem and Wewak town on the 27th. While encountering no air opposition, there were losses to antiaircraft fire, one B-25 from the 823rd and one from the 498th Bomb Squadron with both crews being lost. On the following day, 23 43rd Bomb Group B-24Ds hit Wewak dispersal areas and 24 90th Bomb Group B-24Ds slammed Boram. Results were good, but heavy antiaircraft fire caused damage to several 90th aircraft.

The 4th Air Army was not idle during this time despite its losses during the previous two months. Primary targets were the Allies' Markham and Ramu Valley airfields that threatened 18th Army rear areas, and Allied troops on the Huon Peninsula. However, despite Allied reconnaissance photography showing 82 twin-engined aircraft at Hollandia on November 19, bombers were at a premium, since the Helen regiments had very few operational aircraft and the Lilys of the 45th Air Regiment had already departed by mid-November. Because of fuel shortages, 4th Air Army gave priority to fighter operations. Nonetheless, 14th Air Regiment Sallys, escorted by Oscars, raided Nadzab on November 6 and 7. The raid on the 6th by ten Sallys and ten Oscars was unopposed and two 41st Fighter Squadron P-39Ns were destroyed and 23 other fighters damaged by fragmentation bombs along with two personnel killed and 16 wounded. That same day, several Oscars strafed Nadzab and Gusap; at the latter airfield they destroyed one C-47 and damaged two more without loss to the attackers. The November 7

Kenney and Whitehead kept the pressure on Teramoto. But, Dagua, Wewak, and Boram came in for frequent 5th Air Force attention. Here, 71st Bomb Squadron parafrags descend on Wewak on November 27, 1943, as a 68th Air Regiment Tony burns in its revetment and an unidentified Sally and possible 6th Air Division Dinah stand nearby. (NARA)

raid by nine Sallys escorted by about 30 Oscars of the 13th, 59th, and 248th Air Regiments was contested by four 8th, four 36th, four 341st, and eight 40th Fighter Squadron aircraft conducting morning patrols. In the ensuing engagement, the Sallys bombed and destroyed two P-39s and damaged 12 more, but suffered heavily – two were shot down, three heavily damaged, and four ditched. The escorting fighters from the 248th Air Regiment shot down two 40th P-39Ns, but lost two Oscars with their pilots being killed and had four more crash land at Alexishafen. In addition, the 13th and 59th Air Regiments lost three Oscars to the P-39Ns and P-47Ds. After this costly mission, the 14th Air Regiment was transferred west to Namlea to rebuild. Groups of Japanese fighters made ineffective strafing attacks against Nadzab, Finschhafen, and Huon Peninsula targets. The 7th Air Division, placed under 2nd Area Army in the NEI, moved its headquarters to Ambon on November 21, leaving just Itabana's 6th Air Division under 8th Area Army. IJAAF attacks continued on November 26 when ten 208th Air Regiment Lilys struck Australian positions northwest of Finschhafen from 19,000ft and escaped unscathed. Meanwhile, 20 escorting Oscars shot down two No 4 Squadron Boomerangs flying ground support from Finschhafen, the only two of this type lost in New Guinea during air combat. Afterwards, the Oscars dueled intercepting 35th Fighter Squadron P-40Ns and 35th Fighter Group P-39s, losing four Oscars while downing one 40th Fighter Squadron P-39N. All pilots on both sides were lost.

American attacks on Cape Gloucester intensified starting December 1 when B-24s began conducting twice-daily raids against targets in that area. Again, ADVON called in the 380th Bomb Group to supplement the 43rd and 90th Groups in this effort – 24 of its B-24s were deployed from NWA to Dobodura on December 9 for a four-week deployment. The 5th dropped more than 1,100 tons of bombs between December 1 and 12 on runways, bivouac areas, defensive gun emplacements, barge staging points, and supply dumps. Gasmata was hit severely on December 13 to keep the Japanese off balance, receiving 248 tons of bombs and more than 100,000 machine gun rounds that day from 62 B-24D and 48 B-25D/G sorties. The Arawe area was strafed extensively on December 13 by 34 Kittyhawks of Nos 76 and 78 Squadrons and struck heavily on December 14 by 433 tons of bombs. The B-24D

The IJAAF 248th Air Regiment was in the thick of the fighting from November 1943 to April 1944, staging from Alexishafen and often dueling with 5th Air Force in offensive and defensive missions. Here, one of its wrecked Oscars is examined by US troops at Tadji in April. (NARA)

groups, including the 380th detachment, that day destroyed suspected bivouac and supply areas, while 36 345th Bomb Group B-25s hit jetty areas.

The IJAAF continued to hit back as December unfolded. Many 248th, 68th, and 78th Air Regiment fighters, staging from Madang and Alexishafen, mounted a strafing attack against Ramu Valley airfields on December 10 using the Finisterre Range mountains to conceal their early morning approach. At around 0845hrs, eight 8th Fighter Squadron P-40Ns patrolling near Dumpu were alerted by the Third Air Task Force controller at Gusap to approaching enemy fighters at 9,500ft and 14,000ft. In a dogfight among broken clouds, the 8th and 9th Squadrons, the latter having transferred its new P-47Ds from Dobodura to Gusap that very morning, headed off the attack and claimed four Tonys destroyed for one P-40N severely damaged. The 7th Fighter Squadron, returning from a Hansa Bay sweep, ran into the gaggle of Oscars and Tonys returning to Alexishafen at 0920hrs and in a quick skirmish claimed a Tony and Oscar for another P-40N crash landed at Gusap. Nine Helens targeted Gusap again on December 12. They dropped bombs from 11,000ft, causing only slight damage. Intercepted by 7th Fighter Squadron P-40Ns and 9th Fighter Squadron P-47Ds just after their attack, one Helen was shot down by a P-40N; three P-40Ns were seriously damaged by the tail guns of the fleeing bombers. Oscars from the escorting 248th Air Regiment damaged another P-40N that was written off after crash landing at Gusap, while losing one Oscar.

Dexterity began on December 15 at 0530hrs when elements of the 112th Calvary Regiment landed at Arawe. The landing itself was unopposed by Japanese air power, though the assault force had been detected enroute at around 0300hrs by a 958 Air Group Aichi E13A Jake reconnaissance seaplane from Rabaul. Despite being sighted at around 0800hrs by New Britain coastwatchers and being detected by radar on *Reid*, an IJNAF raid of eight Bettys and 56 Zeros managed to elude 16 covering P-38Hs due to heavy clouds and attacked at about 0900hrs. The attack lasted only a few minutes and resulted in no damage to any ships, but some small craft were damaged and supplies ashore destroyed. Japanese aviators claimed

A 7th Fighter Squadron P-40N runs up at Gusap for takeoff in November 1943 with the operations hut in the background. The 49th Fighter Group shared the base with the 312th Bomb Group when the latter's P-40s arrived in December. Aircrews considered Gusap one of the better New Guinea bases, due to the area's relatively favorable weather pattern. (NARA)

"half of the landing craft" sunk, but 11th Air Fleet recorded two Bettys and four Zeros lost. An afternoon reconnaissance mission by a 26th Air Regiment Sonia that spotted the invasion force prompted an IJAAF response. The ensuing raid was intercepted by eight 432nd Fighter Squadron P-38s. As the 11 Helens and 44 Oscar and Tony escorts were having trouble with weather east of Finschhafen, the P-38s attacked. In the murk, neither side suffered losses, but the bombers had to settle for an ineffective bombing of Finschhafen's Langemak Bay. On December 16, 17, 18, and 21, both the IJNAF and IJAAF mounted bombing and strafing raids against the Arawe landing area, usually consisting of between five and ten bombers accompanied by 20 to 40 fighters. Each day, the 475th and 348th Fighter Groups intercepted formations of Japanese aircraft identified by the destroyer *Shaw* or other controllers. Total damage to the invasion force was limited to one small transport sunk and one damaged, along with one minesweeper and six LSTs damaged.

The immediate lead-up to Operation *Dexterity*'s main event, the landing of the 1st Marine Division at Cape Gloucester, established the term "Gloucesterizing" within 5th Air Force as a synonym for massive, sustained airborne destruction. The B-24s hit Cape Gloucester targets every day between December 15 and 25; together with supporting attacks from B-25s and B-26s, a daily average of 260 tons of bombs were delivered. Even the shorter-range P-40s/Kittyhawks played an important role by keeping the IJNAF's New Britain staging airfields at Cape Hoskins and Talasea under threat. Japanese supply transports were still targeted day and night, often by recco B-24Ds.

Starting on December 20, RAAF Black Cat Catalinas of Nos 11, 20, and 43 Squadrons made night bombing attacks on targets ranging from Gasmata all the way to Kavieng. The Australians were joined by USN VP-34 Black Cats from Samarai on December 26. USN PBY-5A Black Cats and 63rd Bomb Squadron Snoopers conducted night shipping attacks between Cape Gloucester and Kavieng; an XB-24 conducting weather reconnaissance on December 14 was probably lost to a 251 Air Group Irving near Gasmata. Despite the attention paid to Cape Gloucester, ADVON did not forget the threat from the IJAAF. The Second and Third Air Task Forces directed bombers and fighters to hit Wewak on December 22 when the 345th Bomb Group sent 36 B-25s over Wewak and Boram in two waves as clouds gathered. Along with intense antiaircraft fire, about 30 Oscars and Tonys from four regiments provided the opposition. The Japanese fighters, patrolling over a resupply convoy, dove on the bombers, shooting down four B-25s and badly damaging

Reccos flew virtually daily and were often contested. On December 23 about 1710hrs, this radar-equipped 403rd Bomb Squadron recco attacked a transport near Wewak. Two reacting fighters and antiaircraft fire severely damaged the plane and mortally wounded a crewman. It later crash-landed in the Ramu Valley where Australian troops inspect it. (AWM)

These 499th Bomb Squadron B-25s, each carrying 22 100lb demolition bombs, fly over the Cape Gloucester invasion force at about 0720hrs on December 26. The 345th Bomb Group bombed and strafed the Yellow Beach landing zone just after the USN bombardment lifted and just before the Marines began hitting the beach. (NARA)

several more. The Japanese fighters made only one pass before 34 8th and 475th Fighter Group P-38s caught them and claimed 16 for two 80th Fighter Squadron P-38s shot down (pilots lost) and one 431st Fighter Squadron P-38 crash landed. The Japanese claimed four B-25s and four P-38s in exchange for eight aircraft lost with four pilots killed. The 38th Bomb Group hit But and Dagua on December 23 in bad weather with several fires observed. Four 341st Fighter Squadron P-47Ds were on a sweep over Dagua at about the same time and claimed one Tony, but Japanese records indicate no losses. The 5th also hit IJAAF staging bases at Madang and Alexishafen over ten days between December 19 and 31.

A probable Dinah spotted the Cape Gloucester invasion convoy at around 1300hrs on December 25 and reported it to 11th Air Fleet before being shot down by a patrolling 35th Fighter Squadron P-40N. However, the Japanese assessed incorrectly that the convoy was heading for Arawe. The morning of December 26 was clear, though clouds developed as the day progressed. The First Air Task Force planned preparatory attacks in conjunction with a USN bombardment of the landing area. First, 43 B-24s bombed "Target Hill," an elevation overlooking the main landing beach, after destroyer guns pounded the shore. The B-24s were followed by 345th Bomb Group B-25s covering Japanese positions on Target Hill with white phosphorous smoke, while bombing and strafing the landing area. After the landings at 0745hrs, the 89th Bomb Squadron was on alert to provide direct support. More B-24s bombed Target Hill and other elevations later in the day, while the 38th Bomb Group strafed the beach area. The landing was a complete success; by December 29, the Marines had captured Cape Gloucester's two airstrips.

Despite having misread the destination of the invasion force, the Japanese began heavy air attacks with both IJNAF and IJAAF units that afternoon. First Air Task Force planned fighter patrols over the invasion area from 0630hrs to 1830hrs to meet any challenge. At about 1420hrs, the afloat air controller on the *Shaw* plotted a large formation coming from Rabaul and provided intercept vectors to the 80th, 431st, 35th, and 36th Fighter Squadrons. The IJNAF attackers numbered 25 Vals and 63 Zeros in two groups, and before they could be intercepted by the fighters, at least ten Vals executed a successful attack on ships inside the offshore reef. The destroyer *Brownson* was sunk and destroyers *Shaw*, *Lamson*, and *Mugford*

Beginning around 1445hrs on December 26 the IJNAF attacked the Cape Gloucester invasion force for about 25 minutes, sinking a destroyer and damaging three more along with two LSTs. Here, an LST's Coast Guard gunners try to ward off the attackers with their Oerlikon 20mm cannon as two near-miss bombs explode in the background. (NARA)

were damaged, along with two LSTs. In the ensuing air battle, American fighters claimed 22 Vals and 24 Zeros for the loss of two P-38s and two P-47s. Actual Japanese losses were 13 Vals and four Zeros, the surviving Vals having escaped by flying at very low altitude from the target area. That same afternoon at about 1700hrs, the 348th Fighter Group broke up an IJAAF attack before it could inflict any damage. Fourteen of 15 7th and 61st Air Regiment Helens, virtually the entire 4th Air Army heavy bomber force, were shot down – none of the 13 escorting 248th Air Regiment Oscars was lost. During these two attacks, American antiaircraft gunners accounted for two 345th B-25s and one 348th P-47 while shooting down only one Val.

After capturing the two airstrips at Cape Gloucester, the Allies found them to be unsuitable for large-scale operations. Heavy rain delayed use of the airfields by C-47s until February 1, and thereafter they were only briefly used by the 8th Fighter Group and RAAF Kittyhawks. The real benefit of the invasion was providing for the security of Allied naval operations in the Vitiaz and Dampier Straits, because the Allies had airfields on both sides of the straits. IJNAF nighttime harassment attacks on Cape Gloucester occurred intermittently until the last on February 13, 1944, when a 751 Air Group Betty dropped four bombs, killing seven personnel and destroying an amphibious tractor.

Meanwhile, NWA units kept the pressure on. The 2nd Area Army implemented a building plan for airfields to support the defensive line IGHQ was drawing through western New Guinea, and 4th Air Army replacement aircraft were staging through airfields there from the NEI. Nos 11, 20, and 43 Squadron Black Cats, now also flying from Darwin, conducted reconnaissance along with mining and shipping attacks, while the 380th Bomb Group and Nos 2, 18, and 31 Squadrons periodically struck IJAAF and IJNAF airfields, supply nodes, shipping, and infrastructure in the NEI. While some of its B-24s were deployed to Dobodura to support *Dexterity*, the 380th continued long-range strikes against IJN and IJA and strategic NEI targets, but it also hit priority targets on New Guinea such as Manokwari, Babo, and Sorong to disrupt resupply for 4th Air Army and 18th Army.

Force levels for both sides changed in early 1944. New units joined 5th Air Force, and some units departed to undergo aircraft conversions. All 3rd Bomb Group squadrons converted to A-20Gs at Nadzab by February 1, the 22nd Bomb Group converted to the

Thirteen 380th Bomb Group B-24s heading for 23rd Air Flotilla headquarters at Kendari on January 8, 1944, came under attack from IJNAF 202 Air Group Zeros (one circled), losing one B-24. The 530th Bomb Squadron B-24D pictured was lost with its crew four days later on a night mission over Balikpapan to a 202 Air Group Irving night fighter. (NARA)

B-24 at Nadzab between January and early March, the 312th Bomb Group's squadrons converted from P-40Ns to A-20Gs from mid-January until late February, and the 35th Fighter Group converted to P-47Ds. The 345th Bomb Group's B-25s moved from Port Moresby into Nadzab by late February. The 58th Fighter Group, flying P-47Ds, began operations from Dobodura by February 1. The 20th Combat Mapping Squadron joined the 6th Photo Reconnaissance Group, and the 71st Reconnaissance Group added the 110th Reconnaissance Squadron (Fighter) and the 25th Liaison Squadron. The 20th's F-7As, configured for very long-range photo missions, arrived at Nadzab by February 14. The 110th flew ground support with its P-39Ns from Gusap starting on January 20, while the 25th soon became a jack-of-all-trades unit that ADVON found indispensable. Kenney's second night fighter squadron, the 421st, arrived at Nadzab on February 1, but did not begin missions until late that month due to lack of aircraft. Also in February, 5th Air Force received 58 P-38Js with a 55gal gas tank in each wing's leading edge. At Kenney's direction, the 4th Air Depot Group at Townsville and 482nd Service Squadron at Nadzab undertook to modify 56 and 37 older P-38s, respectively, by late March with wing tank kits supplied from the US. No 10 Operational Group filled out its No 77 Wing when Nos 21 and 23 Squadrons, flying Vengeances, arrived at Nadzab in February to begin ground support missions.

After the landings at Arawe and Cape Gloucester, 8th Area Army requested that IGHQ send three additional air regiments, two fighter and one bomber, to New Guinea. The 4th Air Army received the 63rd Air Regiment in early January at Wewak. But the 7th Air Regiment departed with its five remaining Helens from New Guinea by January 17, leaving the 61st at Wakde as the only "heavy" bomber unit in the 4th's inventory. Replacement aircraft continued to arrive. The 7th Air Division at Ambon reported that as of January 24 the 5th Air Regiment had 34 Nicks on hand, the 13th possessed 17 Nicks, and the 75th had 41 Lilys. There were another 120 aircraft of various types at Manila on January 28 awaiting delivery to their final destinations. The 4th Air Army reported on February 2 having 22 Oscars, one Tony, one Nick, 13 Dinahs, 15 Lilys, 28 Helens, and two Sonias at Hollandia, though it is unclear whether these were operational or represented aircraft held in reserve.

The 71st Tactical Reconnaissance Group's 25th Liaison Squadron began operations in January 1944 from Nadzab. Its Stinson L-5 Sentinels, mostly piloted by senior enlisted men, performed tactical reconnaissance, artillery spotting, downed pilot rescue, and light cargo and personnel transport. Here local people prepare to load supplies for delivery to an Allied reconnaissance patrol somewhere in the jungle. (NARA)

Saidor was MacArthur's next target. Its seizure would cut off 18th Army forces still ensconced around Sio from their supply center at Madang. An amphibious assault was quickly arranged using elements of the US 32nd Infantry Division not needed at Cape Gloucester. The landing was executed early on January 2. Although bad weather that morning washed out planned 5th Air Force fighter cover, a few bombers hit suspected IJA positions behind the landing area while the assault force discharged more than 7,000 troops with their supplies and quickly departed to avoid air attacks. The IJAAF mounted an attack that afternoon when seven Helens and an unknown number of Lilys, escorted by more than 30 Oscars and Tonys, headed for the landing area. Eleven 7th Fighter Squadron P-40Ns on a sweep to Madang encountered the inbound Japanese raid at 1610hrs, about 40 miles northwest of Saidor. While the fighters from both sides mixed it up, the Japanese bombers made their attack with minimal success. Some equipment ashore was damaged, but the Japanese aviators claimed one transport set afire and three small boats sunk. Two Helens, a 248th Oscar, and a 78th Tony were destroyed against the loss of one P-40N with its pilot killed. The IJAAF and IJNAF made 49 additional attacks against the Saidor area during the following month, mostly nighttime harassing attacks that caused very little damage.

The Allies' next moves in the air campaign were determined after the exploitation of IJA cipher material acquired by New Guinea Force after the IJA 20th Division abandoned Sio in January. This intelligence indicated that 18th Army perceived Madang and Hansa Bay as the next Allied objectives. The Japanese also planned to build up manpower and air power in the Admiralty Islands. Accordingly, Teramoto deployed 12 63rd Air Regiment Oscars to Momote on January 22. After Saidor was captured, *Reno IV* had originally called for a landing at Hansa Bay. ADVON directed most of the bomber and many fighter missions in January against Alexishafen, Madang, and Bogadjim to support the Allied ground push westward from the Huon Peninsula and Saidor by starving the IJA of supplies. Targets around these locations were bombed on 25 days in January, as well as the road between Bogadjim and Sio along which IJA supplies were carried. Maritime traffic between Hansa Bay and Saidor was also bombed and strafed repeatedly. All Japanese airfields within range of the upcoming SWPA assault objectives received attention. These

A reconnaissance photo of Momote airfield, called by Kenney (with some hyperbole) "the most important piece of real estate in the theater." The Allies considered the Admiralties' facilities excellent for air and sea power projection. [Inset] Damaged 63rd Air Regiment Oscars sit at Momote's southern end after the January 24 attack by B-25s. (NARA)

included Momote and Lorengau in the Admiralties, which were struck on four days between January 22 and 27. On both January 22 and 24, the 345th Bomb Group's B-25s conducted attacks, the first day on shipping and supply dumps, destroying some barges and damaging the 3,462-ton *Koan Maru* off Los Negros. On January 24, the group hit Momote and destroyed eight of 12 63rd Air Regiment Oscars along with finishing off the *Koan Maru* and destroying the 500-ton *Tatsu Maru*, four barges, and a small craft. None of the 345th's aircraft was lost but several received damage from antiaircraft fire. A strike at about noon the next day by 64 B-25s of the 38th and 345th Bomb Groups cost two 345th aircraft; one ditched crew was saved by a USN PBY-5A. On January 26 and 27, both the 43rd and 90th Bomb Groups bombed Momote and Lorengau airfields and other targets on Manus Island with no losses.

Wewak continued to loom large in Kenney's threat perception. Contributing to this was ongoing aggressive IJAAF fighter activity. Examples included a January 15 IJAAF fighter attack on forward Allied airfields. Nineteen Oscars of the 59th and 248th Air Regiments and 12 Tonys of the 68th and 78th strafed Gusap and Nadzab. At Gusap, a 3rd Bomb Group A-20 suffered bomb damage and two 9th Fighter Squadron P-47Ds were set afire, while at Nadzab four 35th Fighter Group P-47Ds sustained minor damage. The next day, a force of about 60 aircraft comprising Tonys from the 68th Air Regiment and Oscars from the 59th, 63rd, and 248th Air Regiments attacked the Saidor beachhead as a resupply convoy approached. Fifteen 35th Fighter Squadron P-40Ns covering the convoy engaged as some Japanese fighters released their bombs. At about the same time, an estimated 30 68th Tonys intercepted a 38th Bomb Group attack on roads and villages along the coast near Madang. Although 16 escorting 433rd Fighter Squadron P-38s intervened, the Tonys still managed to attack the 71st Bomb Squadron. These two engagements resulted in one B-25 shot down and damage to three P-40Ns and three P-38s for the loss of ten Japanese fighters, seven to the P-40Ns and three to the B-25's return fire.

While the 5th's fighters made several sweeps over the Wewak area in January, the heavies only hit Wewak and Boram airfields three times, on January 19, 23, and 24. The raid on the 23rd prompted a big clash as 51 Tonys and Oscars met 35 B-24s in aggressive head-on attacks. The escort, consisting of 27 8th and 475th Group P-38s and 29 49th P-40s, engaged the Japanese resulting in six Japanese aircraft lost for four P-38s and one P-40. Kenney's plan was to temporarily ignore But and Dagua to make the IJAAF more comfortable operating from those airfields. The 5th Air Force was building up for another massive attack against the Wewak-area airfields ahead of the Admiralties landing, scheduled for April 1.

Kenney's big blow came on February 3 with a two-wave attack to maximize IJAAF losses. That morning ADVON launched the first wave of 58 43rd and 90th Bomb Group B-24s that hit Wewak and Boram airstrips and dispersal areas at about 1130hrs. Thirty-two escorting 348th P-47Ds warded off approximately 30 Oscars and Tonys of the 59th, 63rd, 78th, and 248th Air Regiments, claiming eight destroyed for no losses and no B-24s damaged. The second wave consisted of 17 7th Fighter Squadron P-40Ns and 15 432nd Fighter Squadron P-38s escorting 27 38th Bomb Group and 41 345th Bomb Group B-25D/Gs to hit But and Dagua airfields, respectively. The B-25s arrived at about 1200hrs, and although Wewak passed an air raid warning, the strafers caught the IJAAF fighters that had challenged the first wave on the ground, having landed at different fields because of damage at Wewak and Boram. Although nine assorted Tonys, Oscars, and Nicks patrolled over the airfields, they were engaged by the escorts and never reached the B-25s. The B-25s proceeded to strafe and bomb the airstrips, antiaircraft sites, dispersal areas, supply dumps, and bivouac areas with parafrags and parademos, causing considerable destruction. Only six 38th Bomb Group aircraft were damaged by antiaircraft fire with three aircrew wounded. Their escorts shot down an Oscar along with six Lilys trying to land at But. Altogether, the IJAAF acknowledged the loss that day of 57 aircraft destroyed or damaged while 5th Air Force lost no attacking aircraft. Kenney insisted Wewak's airfields be "kept beaten down" in the lead-up to the Admiralties assault, so ADVON paid them additional attention during the month. The Wewak area was bombed or strafed on February 4, 10, 12, 23, 24, 26, and 27, and fighter sweeps were flown in the area.

After the February 3 debacle, 4th Air Army was once again in desperate straits. As of February 10, Teramoto possessed only 60 flyable aircraft of all types, including just 21 Oscars

On February 3, 1944, 5th Air Force made a two-pronged attack on Wewak's airfields. In this view early in the attack on Dagua, 11 fatally exposed 68th and 78th Air Regiment Tonys (top), three unidentified Helens, and four 248th Air Regiment Oscars (bottom) await destruction. Explosions erupt (top left and right) while parademos descend (left). (NARA)

and eight Tonys; by the 22nd, his fighter force was reduced to only eight Oscars and six Tonys. The exhausted 59th Air Regiment departed for Japan on February 17, but the fresh 33rd and 77th Air Regiments transferred to New Guinea by February 26. This gave 4th Air Army's six fighter regiments a total strength of 83: 24 Oscars in the 33rd, 18 Oscars in the 63rd, 20 Oscars in the 77th, and three Oscars in the 248th; the 68th had eight Tonys and the 78th had ten. The 34th Air Regiment also arrived at Hollandia on February 19 with 15 Lilys, and the 61st Air Regiment's 15 Helens at Wakde were supplemented with 15 Sallys. The 45th Air Regiment's Lilys were joined by some Nicks configured as fighter-bombers. Including reconnaissance and transport planes, Teramoto could count on 170 operational aircraft by month's end. At the same time, the Allies estimated that Hollandia's three main airfields held 277 aircraft, 132 of them fighters.

The Allies continued to fly hundreds of missions supporting the American and Australian pincers pushing westward. Between February 2 and 9, A-20s and B-25s hit various targets in the Alexishafen and Madang areas. After a mid-month interlude during which it was focused on SOPAC support, the 5th again attacked targets around Hansa Bay, Madang, and Alexishafen with A-20s and B-25s on eight days between February 21 and 29. No 10 Operational Group also intensified its ground support in the Markham and Ramu Valleys with the newly arrived Nos 21 and 23 Squadrons' Vengeances, altogether dropping 200 tons of bombs on IJA positions by February 29. Also in late February, RAAF crews began flying B-24 missions with the 65th Bomb Squadron. This was a result of an agreement Kenney made in January that the RAAF should acquire B-24s. After preliminary work-ups at Charters Towers, RAAF crews were assigned to both the 43rd and 380th Bomb Groups and flew many missions in preparation for receiving B-24s later in 1944.

However, the encirclement of Rabaul was still incomplete. SOPAC planned to take Nissan in the Green Islands on February 15, only 115nm from Rabaul. The 5th Air Force assisted by attacking airfields and shipping around New Britain, New Ireland, and New Hanover on several days. On February 11, 48 43rd and 90th Bomb Group B-24s, escorted by P-38s, dropped 170 tons of bombs on Kavieng's airfield and revetments as IJNAF planes were warming up. A raid the next day by 35 B-24s left Kavieng's airfield unusable, and 43 B-24s hit New Ireland's Panapai airfield on February 14. On the 15th, B-25s of the 38th and 345th Bomb Groups and A-20s of the 3rd Bomb Group joined the assault on Kavieng. They hit ammunition and fuel dumps, shipping and dock facilities, but lost six B-25s and two A-20s to antiaircraft fire and flying debris. Fortunately for the Americans, a VP-34 Dumbo from Samarai, covered for a time by four 348th Fighter Group P-47Ds, managed to rescue 15 downed aircrew. By February 20, the IJNAF had withdrawn all but a very few operational aircraft from Rabaul and Kavieng to Truk. A March 12 JCS directive confirmed that Kavieng would not be directly assaulted, so SOPAC substituted Emirau, 75nm from Kavieng. After SOPAC forces took Emirau on March 20, Rabaul, with its almost 100,000 personnel garrison, was, in MacArthur's phrase, allowed to "wither on the vine."

Earlier in February, plans to seize both Kavieng and Hansa Bay were still active, but Kenney thought this would be unnecessary if the Admiralties were captured. The 5th flew several unopposed raids to soften up the IJA's 38th Division's positions on Los Negros and Manus in February, though many sorties failed due to adverse weather. Kenney directed a special "loitering" reconnaissance of Los Negros on February 23 by three 17th Reconnaissance Squadron B-25Ds and used the negative results to talk MacArthur into authorizing a "reconnaissance in force" earlier than the previously planned April 1 Admiralties assault.

After air attacks on Los Negros every day between February 24 and 28, on February 29 elements of the US 1st Cavalry Division executed a hurriedly planned landing. Bad weather

The 5th Air Force targeted Kavieng and surrounding areas in support of SOPAC's invasion of the Green Islands. On February 16, 345th Bomb Group B-25s attacked this CH 28-class subchaser escorting a convoy off New Hanover. A bomb falls toward the ship as at least six Japanese sailors scramble for cover on the forward deck. The ship later grounded on a reef and its crew was strafed as they tried to get ashore. (MacArthur Memorial)

thwarted a thorough air support plan and very little of it was executed. Eight 65th Bomb Squadron B-24s managed to get through the weather ahead of the landing and bombed the assault area at 0738hrs. The heavy bombers proceeded to drop to 400ft altitude to strafe machine gun positions firing on the assault force as it came ashore at 0815hrs. Three 71st Bomb Squadron B-25s also managed to arrive at about 0840hrs and bombed IJA gun positions on the landing zone flanks along with six 345th Bomb Group B-25s that bombed IJA positions behind the landing zone. The next day, eight 433rd Troop Carrier Group transport-configured B-17s flying from Finschhafen dropped additional ammunition to the force. B-24s of the 43rd Bomb Group hit Lorengau on Manus Island while B-25s of the 345th and 38th Bomb Groups hit Los Negros and Manus targets, respectively. The 4th Air Army tried to respond on March 2 with a sweep over the Admiralties by 21 fighters of the 63rd, 248th, and 68th Air Regiments. Although the Tonys got a few shots at 499th Bomb Squadron B-25s making a run on Los Negros and the Oscars mixed it up with six 341st Fighter Squadron P-47Ds just south of Manus, no planes on either side were reported lost. There were no more significant IJAAF challenges in the Admiralties.

After Allied troops were firmly established on Los Negros, ADVON ordered the three fighter squadrons of RAAF No 73 Wing to relocate from Kiriwina to Momote during March to provide support to the ground troops as well as air defense, as the airfields and harbor facilities were readied to support large Allied air and sea forces.

Other major developments affecting RAAF operations followed. First, Kenney assigned No 9 Operational Group to Bostock's RAAF Command, along with operational responsibility for Milne Bay and Port Moresby. He next appointed Air Cmdre Scherger air task force commander for the upcoming Aitape operation. Kenney also ordered No 77 Wing's three Vengeance squadrons back to Australia after March 8 to free up dispersal space for other

ADVON ordered three RAAF fighter squadrons shifted to the Admiralties to cover US ground and maritime operations. Accordingly, these No 76 Squadron Kittyhawks were the first Allied aircraft based at Momote, arriving on March 9. Sister No 73 Wing squadrons Nos 77 (Kittyhawks) and 79 (Spitfires) arrived by March 28. (AWM)

units at Nadzab. Nos 4, 22, 30, and 100 Squadrons were transferred from No 9 Operational Group's control to restock No 10's No 77 Wing. In March, No 10 Operational Group headquarters moved to Cape Gloucester with Nos 75, 78, and 80 Squadrons and took over from the 8th Fighter Group to support ongoing Marine ground operations on New Britain. Their Kittyhawks could operate better from Cape Gloucester's muddy airstrips than the P-38, to which the entire 8th Fighter Group was transitioning. During March and early April, these RAAF squadrons supported the Marines and US Sixth Army operations by hitting Japanese targets between Arawe and Cape Hoskins.

Whitehead moved ADVON forward from Port Moresby to Nadzab by February 20. At the same time, ADVON was busy moving the units from Port Moresby and Dobodura forward as fast as airfield space could be developed to support the final phase of the campaign. The idea was to position the shorter-range fighters (P-40/P-47) and bombers (A-20) farthest forward. The three conventional 43rd Bomb Group squadrons moved into Nadzab by March 14; the 63rd's Snoopers followed in April. The 90th Bomb Group was at Nadzab in February and the 22nd resumed operations with B-24s from there on March 10. Additionally, the 312th Bomb Group's 386th Squadron resumed operations from Gusap on February 25 after re-equipping with the A-20G; its fellow 312th Bomb Group squadrons followed during March. The 35th Fighter Group's P-47Ds relocated to Gusap from Nadzab by mid-February. Other changes to the order of battle included moving the 8th Fighter Group to Nadzab from Cape Gloucester by March 25 and the 475th Fighter Group from Dobodura to Nadzab by March 29. The 6th Reconnaissance Group's F-5 squadrons also moved to Nadzab in mid-March, while the 17th Reconnaissance Squadron's B-25s remained at Finschhafen. The last bomber unit to join the 5th, the 417th Bomb Group, arrived at Dobodura with A-20G, H, and K models in February. Both it and the 58th Fighter Group would move to Saidor by mid-April.

Stepping stones to the Philippines – Hollandia to Sansapor

As consolidation of the seizure of the Admiralties proceeded during March, the Allies refocused on New Guinea itself. Barge traffic, though dwindling, remained a prime target for fighters and medium bombers alike. During March and April, Allied medium bombers and fighters flew hundreds of missions along the coast between Bogadjim and Hansa Bay hunting supply barges, dumps, roads and bridges, and other logistics-related targets to support the ground troops slogging their way westward. Hansa Bay targets were attacked on ten days during March, and ADVON launched a series of attacks on the Wewak area to reinforce the Japanese leadership's estimate that either Hansa Bay or Wewak was MacArthur's next assault target.

Temporarily deploying 24 380th Bomb Group aircraft from NWA to Nadzab on February 28, ADVON directed raids against the Wewak area on 20 days in March, when aircraft availability and weather permitted. Due to deteriorating weather, on March 7 only the 380th made it through to Dagua. Bombing results through the overcast were unobserved, but the group claimed seven possible 63rd Air Regiment Oscars shot down for the loss of one B-24 and crew and two B-24s badly damaged. The 380th returned to NWA two days later. Thereafter, the weather improved and subsequent raids comprised dozens of escorted B-24s and medium bombers.

The 4th Air Army kept doggedly resisting. In March, Teramoto's six fighter regiments were tactically paired under the 14th Air Brigade as three units, mainly due to declining numbers of available aircraft: the 63rd and 248th, the 33rd and 77th, and the 68th and 78th Air Regiments generally flew together. From March 11 to 16, intercepts involving every air regiment but the 248th met Allied raids that targeted airfields, antiaircraft positions, fuel and supply dumps, and buildings, as well as targets on nearby Muschu and Kairiru Islands. The pattern was well practiced: B-24s struck antiaircraft batteries while B-25 and A-20 strafers flew in later at low altitude and bombed and shot up everything else. The 30 to 50 defending Japanese fighters aloft each day only rarely took on the bombers, since the escorting American fighters were so numerous, and vicious dogfights ensued. Total results for these engagements were 36 4th Air Army fighters destroyed in air combat for the loss of one 320th Bomb Squadron B-24, six 90th Bomb Squadron A-20s, one 387th Bomb Squadron A-20, one 40th Fighter Squadron P-47, two 41st Fighter Squadron P-47s, and two 36th Fighter Squadron P-38s. After mid-March, 4th Air Army flew no more large-formation defensive missions from Wewak.

ULTRA intelligence revealed IJA plans for a series of convoys between mid-February and late March 1944 to Rabaul, Wewak, and Hollandia. Of these, it was the Allies' total destruction of the 21st Wewak Area Resupply Convoy on March 18 and 19 that essentially sealed the fate of 18th Army's forward defenses. During the night of March 18–19, a 63rd Bomb Squadron Snooper detected the convoy on radar heading from Hollandia to Wewak. The convoy consisted of two transports, a small freighter, and three subchaser escorts. The XB-24 descended from 4,000ft to 1,500ft and made two passes, damaging one transport, before returning to base. The ships used searchlights and began firing, damaging the Snooper.

Rare photo of a 63rd Bomb Squadron all-black XB-24 "Snooper" with engines turning. The XB-24 carried the secret Low Altitude Bombardment radar/electronic system linked to the autopilot and Norden bombsight. Beginning in October 1943 the squadron mainly conducted night attacks against Japanese shipping, such as that against the Wewak resupply convoy, but also flew important night reconnaissance/ pathfinder missions. (AWM)

Later that morning, the Allies found the convoy making 15kts about 50nm from Wewak heading back to Hollandia. It had discharged its cargo at Wewak overnight and was steaming back to Hollandia with about 1,000 4th Air Army personnel and an air search radar unit and equipment. Several B-24s of the 22nd, 43rd, and 90th Bomb Groups, diverting from airfield targets, attacked the convoy from between 9,000ft and 12,000ft. The convoy was not covered by fighters, although about 28 33rd, 77th, and 78th Air Regiment fighters that opposed a concurrent raid against the nearby airfields did attack some of the bombers. The B-24s claimed a subchaser sunk and damage to the *Taiei Maru* and the *Yakumo Maru*. The 22nd endured attacks by about six fighters, but fought them off with three of its B-24s damaged. One fighter was claimed as destroyed and two were damaged. That afternoon, about 80 3rd and 345th Bomb Group aircraft attacked the remnants of the convoy. The 3rd lost two A-20s to antiaircraft fire with only one man of either crew being saved. No 345th aircraft were lost, but at least three 500th Bomb Squadron B-25Ds were hit by *Taiei Maru*'s antiaircraft fire. The two bomb groups finished off the two transports and two subchasers. Destruction of the convoy caused IGHQ to indefinitely postpone supply convoys to Wewak, leaving 18th Army's 50,000 troops to get supplies from Hollandia. However, with the Allies strangling barge traffic along the coast, very little materiel from Hollandia reached the front-line forces.

Raids on Wewak continued until the end of March when Kenney's declared Wewak "finished off" as the center of IJAAF operations in New Guinea. Teramoto apparently agreed, because he moved his headquarters to Hollandia on March 25. Between March 11 and 27, 5th Air Force's 1,543 bomber sorties delivered 3,036 tons of bombs on Wewak-area targets. The area's infrastructure was a shambles and the airfields could only be fully repaired with great difficulty. Kenney could now turn his full attention to Hollandia. Major IJA base facilities were located there, and the area included four airfields: Hollandia, Cyclops, Sentani, and Tami, though Tami was not yet operational. Hollandia was an important staging area for sea and air transport to garrisons further east, as well as having become 18th Army's principal logistics center. Immense amounts of supplies were located there. Despite its importance, the garrison was weak – 15,000 total personnel of which 80 percent were in non-combat service units.

Kenney's preparations for the Hollandia assault began even as the Admiralties were still being cleared of Japanese troops. The RAAF's No 73 Wing's fighters had relocated to Momote

The Japanese used the 21st Wewak Resupply Convoy to reprovision 18th Army, then tried to transfer about 1,000 4th Air Army personnel from Wewak to Hollandia. On March 19, 5th Air Force destroyed the convoy as it left Wewak. Here the 3,221-ton *Taiei Maru* lists under attack by 90th Bomb Squadron A-20Gs. (NARA)

in March. On March 25 and 26, VP-33 moved to Seeadler Bay, joined by fellow Black Cats of Nos 11 and 20 Squadrons by April 13 using the *Tangier*, *San Pablo*, and *Heron* seaplane tenders. In addition to the normal shipping strikes, the Catalinas conducted nighttime area reconnaissance and mining of key IJN island ports to hinder Japanese opposition from out of the theater. Also, a VP-34 detachment was deployed to Finschhafen aboard the seaplane tender *Half Moon*. Momote and Lorengau airfields were operational, and Mokerang airfield on Los Negros was ready to accommodate heavy bombers by April 22; XIII Bomber Command that month released the 5th and 307th Bomb Groups, including its 868th Bomb Squadron Snoopers, to move to the Admiralties. Kenney, on April 11, appointed Maj. Gen. Streett to head 13th Air Task Force, also based there, under ADVON control. These bomb groups were still earmarked for support of Nimitz's thrust and flew several Central Pacific missions. Importantly, these operations also helped to ensure that no Japanese threat to Operation *Reckless* would emanate from the north.

Opening moves in the air campaign against Hollandia consisted of limited night harassment bombings beginning on March 4. Aitape also received attention beginning in mid-March. In fact, while the P-38s were being converted to carry added fuel, the 5th's fighters were forbidden to fly any farther west than Aitape to reinforce Teramoto's perception that escorted, large-scale daylight bombing raids on Hollandia were impossible. However, photographic reconnaissance showed a build-up of antiaircraft positions at Hollandia in March and ULTRA information indicated that Teramoto, despite Kenney's disinformation efforts, might move his aircraft farther west. If this occurred 4th Air Army would again be out of range of the 5th's escort fighters and thus in position to threaten Operation *Reckless*. Since the extended-range P-38 conversion was basically complete by March 27, ADVON directed a series of large-scale attacks on Hollandia, Cyclops, and Sentani airfields to catch Teramoto's aircraft before they escaped.

On March 28 and 29 the 43rd Bomb Group flew a few aircraft each night over the Hollandia coast to drop fragmentation bombs and flares to keep the Japanese awake. During

The 13th Air Force's 5th Bomb Group arrived at Momote by mid-April 1944; its 307th Bomb Group joined it in late May. The 13th's B-24s dropped almost 2,000 tons of bombs between April 18 and May 27 and directly supported the Biak operation. Here a 5th Group B-24J hits Biak on May 9. Note the extended ball turret, something not used on 5th Air Force B-24s. (USAF)

the night of March 29–30, seven aircraft of the 43rd and 90th Bomb Groups hit dispersal areas and conducted weather reconnaissance. At 1035hrs on March 30, 63 B-24s of the 22nd, 43rd, and 90th Bomb Groups, each carrying 240 20lb fragmentation bombs, targeted the dispersal areas at Hollandia's three airfields. Bombing from 10,000ft to 12,500ft was reported as good and only light antiaircraft fire was encountered. About 25 to 30 Oscars of the 33rd, 63rd, and 77th Air Regiments got airborne and attacked the 65th Bomb Squadron, but no losses resulted. The escorting 475th Fighter Group and 80th Fighter Squadron P-38s accounted for eight Oscars destroyed for no loss.

The next day's raid was a repeat performance. Seventy B-24s from the three groups dropped 1,000lb demolition, 20lb fragmentation and incendiary bombs on the three airfields. Again, no B-24s or P-38s were lost, but heavier antiaircraft fire damaged a few bombers. The P-38s claimed 14 kills, but the Japanese recorded only two 33rd Air Regiment Oscars being lost. The 5th estimated the two-day number of aircraft destroyed at 239, but the IJAAF reported "only" 166.

After a two-day hiatus for maintenance and bad weather, the morning of April 3 saw an even heavier blow befall 4th Air Army. Over 300 aircraft plastered Hollandia, Cyclops, and Sentani at about 1050hrs with 66 B-24s dropping 1,000lb demolition bombs from 20,000ft against the airstrips and antiaircraft guns. Within an hour, 96 A-20s and 76 B-25s followed at low altitude, dropping parafrags and parademos, and strafed the airfields, supply dumps, bivouac areas, and ships and facilities at Humboldt and Tanahmerah Bays. The round-trip flight for the twin-engine bombers was demanding from a fuel management perspective, being 1,050 miles from Nadzab and 950 miles from Gusap. The 69 escorting P-38s kept approximately 39 Oscars and Tonys from all but a few passes at the bombers, and the IJAAF

Bombs from 64th Bomb Squadron B-24s explode across Hollandia airfield to open the April 3 attack. Some 4th Air Army aircraft, many already damaged, are just visible scattered around the area. The combination high/low altitude attack that day solidified Allied air supremacy and completely shattered the IJAAF's capability to oppose the Allied campaign in New Guinea. (NARA)

April 3, 1944: massive 5th Air Force attack on 4th Air Army at Hollandia

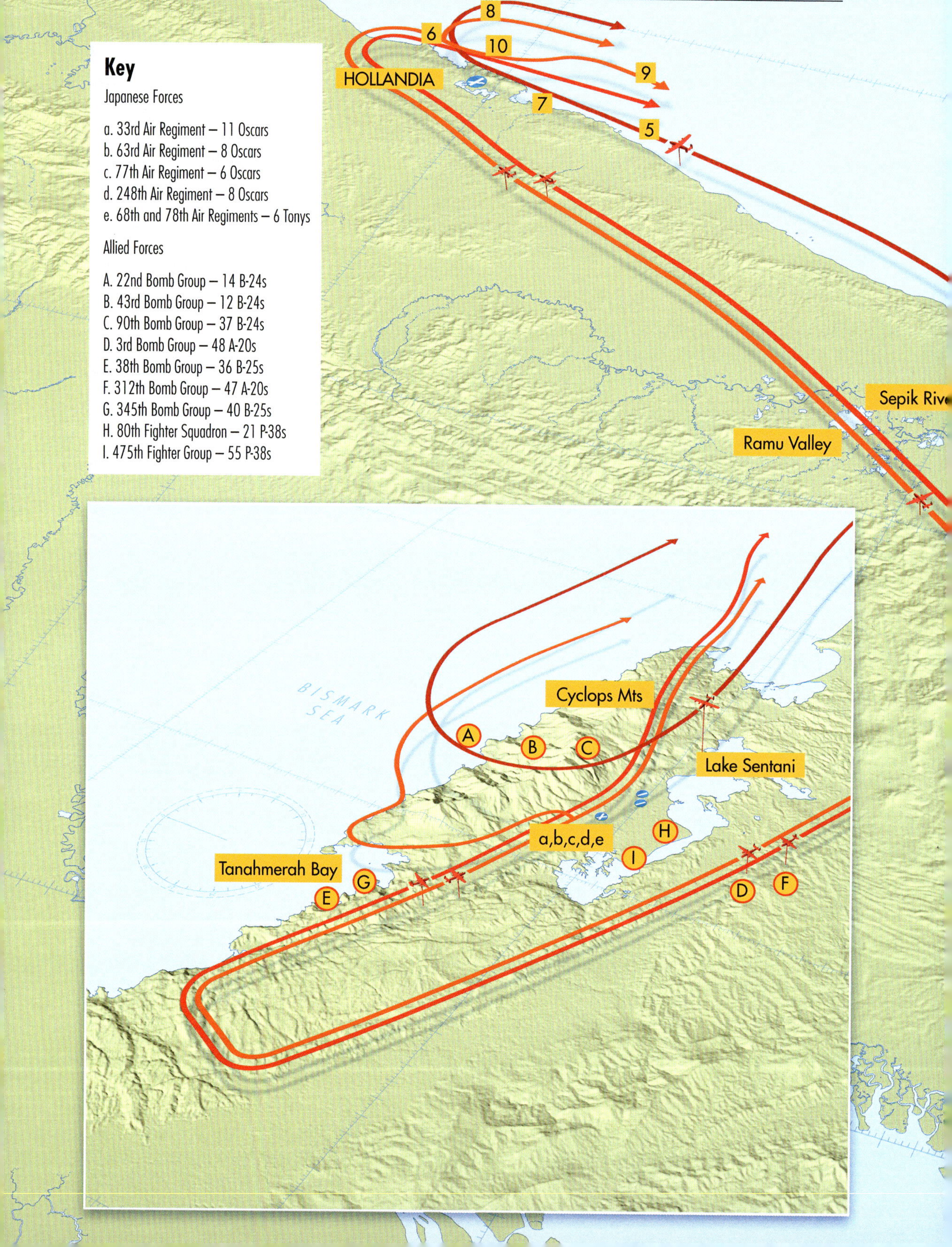

EVENTS

1. B-24s take off from Nadzab around 0810hrs, head northwest at 20,000ft.
2. 80th Fighter Squadron from Nadzab rendezvous with B-24s over Dumpu about 0845hrs for escort, head toward mouth of Sepik River southeast of Wewak.
3. 38th and 345th BG B-25s take off from Nadzab about 0845hrs, 3rd and 312th BG A-20s take off from Gusap about 0850hrs, head for Dumpu at 3,000ft.
4. All medium bombers rendezvous with 475th FG P-38s from Nadzab over Dumpu about 0930hrs, fly over land along Markham and Ramu Valleys toward Hollandia.
5. B-24s begin bombing Hollandia airfields at 1049hrs, striking airstrips, antiaircraft sites and infrastructure. P-38 escort clashes with some of about 39 Oscars and Tonys over the airfields. The B-24s' bomb runs end about 1102hrs and they return to base without loss.
6. The two leading A-20 groups fly past Hollandia to the south and turn back eastward about 25 miles west of the airfields and begin their runs about 1145hrs at 50–100ft over the targets, concentrating on hitting aircraft and supply dumps.
7. P-38 escorts engage remaining fighters between Lake Sentani and the Cyclops mountains.
8. The following two B-25 groups, except for one squadron, follow the same path and begin their attack about 1155hrs. The 500th BS turns northwest and photographs and attacks targets along the road between the airfields and Tanahmerah Bay.
9. By 1202hrs the medium bombers finish their attacks and return directly to base.
10. The P-38s claim 25 destroyed and the bombers two more, but the IJAAF admits losing only 11 in aerial combat. Losses on the ground are estimated to total about 340 aircraft over the three 5th Air Force raids of March 30, 31, and April 3. Many bombers suffer damage from fighters and antiaircraft fire but none are lost. The 432nd Fighter Squadron loses one P-38 and pilot.

lost perhaps as many as 30 aircraft in exchange for the loss of one 432nd Fighter Squadron P-38. The 5th flew a "mop-up" strike on April 5. The result of the onslaught was that 4th Air Army lost as many as 340 aircraft destroyed and more than 2,000 personnel killed.

Following this disaster, Teramoto moved his headquarters from Hollandia to Menado (Manado) in the Celebes on April 15, leaving 6th Air Division with almost nothing to oppose the coming Allied onslaught. On April 20, the 6th reported a total of 23 fighters of the 63rd, 68th, 78th, and 248th Air Regiments operational, along with three probable 34th Air Regiment Lilys, four Dinahs, and two Sonias. After the Allied seizure of Hollandia, most of these units effectively ceased to exist and were formally disbanded by the IJAAF in late July.

After the Hollandia airfields were devastated, later in April ADVON shifted back to hitting Wewak and Hansa Bay to distract from the real *Reckless* objectives. Both areas were struck on seven days between April 5 and 21, and the IJAAF still sometimes challenged the raiders. For example, on April 11, about a dozen fighters, mostly Tonys that staged to Wewak from Hollandia a few days prior, engaged the 8th and 311th Fighter Squadrons covering the 312th and 345th Bomb Groups striking Boram. In the melee, three 311th P-47Ds were lost while the 8th shot down one 78th Air Regiment Tony. The Hollandia area was only targeted four times even though the raids were large. After the April 16 raid, the 5th Air Force suffered its worst one-day loss of the war – to the weather and not the Japanese. Storm fronts closed in on Kenney's forward airfields and fighters and bombers, lost in the murk, made crash landings or ran out of fuel and ditched or crashed in the jungle. On that "Black Sunday," 31 aircraft and 32 aircrew were lost.

For *Reckless*, MacArthur prevailed on the JCS to have Nimitz assign the Pacific Fleet's carrier strike force, Task Force (TF) 58, for air support, since the landing zones were beyond the range of the 5th's fighters. Three task groups of TF 58 were allocated to the operations with five fleet and seven light carriers embarking about 660 aircraft. Nimitz allotted only four days, April 21–24, for his support to the landing. Strikes were planned against Japanese airfields in the Hollandia area and against Wakde and Sarmi further west.

On April 21, carrier and land-based aircraft, estimated to be as many as 600 by the Japanese, worked over facilities around Hollandia with an emphasis on its three main airfields: Hollandia, Cyclops, and Sentani. An unknown number of aircraft were destroyed on the ground. Simultaneous USN air strikes were conducted against Wakde and Sarmi. The TF 58 aircrews did not report a single Japanese aircraft contesting the airspace over Hollandia, only light-to-moderate antiaircraft fire.

Nimitz briefly provided 5th Fleet carrier air cover for the Hollandia assault. This Bombing Squadron Five (VB-5) Douglas SBD-4 Dauntless dive bomber from the TF 58 carrier *Yorktown* loiters protectively over transports carrying two battalions of the 24th Infantry Division heading for the Tanahmerah Bay landing zone (Red Beach 2), where MacArthur himself came ashore. (NARA)

American 41st and 24th Infantry Division troops landed on April 22 at Humboldt Bay and Tanahmerah Bay, respectively, on either end of the coastal Cyclops Mountain Range. No Japanese aircraft opposed the landing that morning. The invasion force moved inland and seized Hollandia's three active airfields on April 26. Because of the IJAAF's weakness, the IJNAF 23rd Air Flotilla was called upon to join the defense. It launched its first attack on the *Reckless* landings the night of April 22, followed by similar attacks on the nights of April 23 and 24. No American ships were hit in these strikes, but a single aircraft on April 23 bombing Humboldt Bay hit an abandoned Japanese ammunition dump, the explosion of which spread to consume landing force supplies accumulated over the previous two days. In addition, 24 men were killed and 100 wounded. The 23rd Air Flotilla strike aircraft were forced to fly an extreme range of 600 miles from Sorong because the torpedoes they carried were not available at Biak. However, Japanese fighter and reconnaissance aircraft were able to use Biak airfields. Elements of the IJAAF 7th Air Division staged from Ambon to Sorong and joined the April 24 attack. The final attack on Allied shipping off Hollandia was conducted on the night of April 27. Aircrew from the 23rd Air Flotilla claimed one light cruiser sunk and another large ship damaged; in fact, no ships were hit.

Concurrently, elements of the US 41st Infantry Division landed at Aitape, about 125 miles east of Hollandia. The 41st was supported by TF 58 aircraft and 11 672nd Bomb Squadron A-20s that bombed and strafed Tadji airfield, the landing force's operational objective eight miles southeast of Aitape. Tadji was captured that day without serious resistance and No 10 Operational Group headquarters moved there. By the afternoon of April 24, No 78 Squadron Kittyhawks were based at Aitape and the airfield was fully operational by April 28. The RAAF fighters flew escort missions for the parade of 317th Troop Carrier Group C-47s bringing in supplies. It was soon determined that, like Hollandia, Tadji's soil was not firm enough for heavy bomber operations, but that lighter aircraft could use the airfield. The 110th Tactical Reconnaissance Squadron's (formerly Reconnaissance Squadron (Fighter)) P-39Ns soon moved to Tadji to fly ground attack against 18th Army elements and No 75 Squadron relocated to Tadji in May, while Nos 78 and 80 Squadrons advanced to Cyclops and were assigned to the 310th Bomb Wing (M). The 49th Fighter Group's two P-40N squadrons also relocated from Gusap to Cyclops in early May. The P-40Ns and Kittyhawks then began escorting B-24 missions to Biak.

The Allies also kept the pressure on the bulk of 18th Army now cut off to the east. Throughout April and May, the Allies continuously pummeled IJA troop positions, supplies, and infrastructure between Wewak and Hansa Bay. Every day between April 23 and May 12, the Allies flew missions in this area, with some attacks lasting throughout the day. Many days saw more than 100 Allied heavy and medium bombers engaged in this effort. This was part of the price paid for bypassing large IJA force concentrations – they had to be kept from mounting any attacks on the various Allied footholds along the New Guinea coast.

Despite 4th Air Army's series of setbacks, Japanese plans for bolstering its position in western New Guinea proceeded. The 7th Air Division again came under 4th Air Army control and braced to resist the Allies after Hollandia. However, the 2nd Area Army's airfield building plan for 1944 had fallen behind schedule due to inadequate construction equipment and only nine airfields were in use. IGHQ ordered the IJA to build more airfields in the Philippines to support the New Guinea forces. The 3rd Air Army in the NEI was also directed to support 4th Air Army with material and maintenance personnel, since so much had been lost at Hollandia.

RAAF squadrons moved from Aitape to Hollandia to support the Biak operation. No 78 Squadron arrived on May 7 and No 78 Wing HQ and No 80 Squadron followed by mid-May. This No 78 Squadron Kittyhawk undergoes maintenance parked next to a derelict 248th Air Regiment Oscar at Cyclops airstrip. (AWM)

Allied softening-up of western New Guinea intensified. Key locations for IJAAF activity were Wakde, Mokmer, Kamiri (Noemfoor), Manokwari, Babo, Mumi, and Nabire, while the IJNAF mainly used Sorong, Fak Fak, and Utarom. Bostock tasked Cole's NWA with striking airfields in the Arafura Sea and western New Guinea. The 380th Bomb Group flew unescorted daylight missions from NWA from early April against targets around Geelvink Bay – dubbed the "Rice Bowl" by the group. The Japanese radar net across western New Guinea gave them around three hours' alert of the 380th's approach and

The 380th Bomb Group flew unescorted daylight raids on western New Guinea from early April on airfields from which the IJAAF and IJNAF could oppose planned Allied westward thrusts. Enemy opposition was sometimes fierce. Here, a probable 5th Air Regiment Nick trails smoke after an encounter with a 380th formation. (AC)

the IJAAF and IJNAF often intercepted these raids. V Bomber Command transferred two "ferret" B-24s, equipped to detect and map these radars, from the 63rd Bomb Squadron to the 380th at this time.

The SWPA was racing not only to get to the Philippines but also to be in position to support Nimitz's thrust in the Marianas planned for early June. Accordingly, Kenney was anxious to seize or develop more suitable bases for heavy bombers farther west. Wakde Island (Insoemoar), 125 miles west of Hollandia, and its coral airstrip was the next objective. The Americans bombed the airstrip out of action by the end of April, but Wakde still received 1,500 more tons up to May 17. Wakde was taken on May 18 after Arare, on the coast opposite, had been seized by 41st Division troops the previous day. The USAAF and RAAF flew sorties for the remainder of May to repulse IJA attacks on US troops around Arare, in some cases using Japanese bombs because Allied ordnance stores at Hollandia were still meager. Wakde was thereafter crowded, hosting the 348th Fighter Group and 17th Reconnaissance Squadron as well as becoming a staging base for other units' aircraft, and it became a tempting Japanese target. Night raids by 23rd Air Flotilla bombers on June 5, 7, and 11 cratered the airstrip and destroyed a fuel dump and 17 aircraft. A detachment of 421st Night Fighter Squadron P-70s, moved forward from Nadzab for defense on May 28, was unable to counter the attacks.

After *Reckless*, Biak became a prime target. The Allies' first daylight raid was made on April 28 by 47 43rd and 90th Bomb Group B-24s. The 5th and 307th Bomb Groups from Momote and Mokerang, respectively, filled in during early May while 5th Air Force heavies at Nadzab were weathered in. Mokmer was reconnoitered and attacked at night by 63rd Bomb Squadron Snoopers from May 9 to 11, and both the 63rd and 868th Bomb Squadrons, staging from Momote, hit the airfield on May 10. Sorido was a 63rd Snooper target from May 12 to 15. May 17 and 22 saw the B-24 groups make additional daylight strikes that caused extensive damage. Concurrently, B-24s and A-20s kept attacking Manokwari, Kamiri, Babo, and Utarom to ensure no enemy aircraft could use these airfields to support the Biak garrison. The 38th Bomb Group even staged its B-25s to Merauke from Nadzab from May 25 to June 5 to focus on Babo.

ADVON prioritized attacks on Japanese airfields in western New Guinea that could threaten the upcoming Biak operation. The 8th Bomb Squadron, staging from Hollandia, sent a dozen A-20Gs against Kamiri on May 21 and claimed at least eight aircraft destroyed, including this Tony caught taxiing in a dispersal area. (NARA)

The IJAAF still had some fight left. From bases in the Halmaheras, Jefman, and Kamiri the 5th, 13th, and 24th Air Regiments flew against the Allied raids in May and June, and the 19th Air Regiment's Tonys, new to the theater and flying from Ambon, entered the waning days of the New Guinea fray in July. The resulting clashes wore these units down until in late July the IJAAF no longer flew over New Guinea.

On May 27, the Americans landed on Biak. The 23rd Air Flotilla and the 7th Air Division committed what few aircraft they had to attack the landing force. On the afternoon of the landing, five IJAAF Nicks loaded with bombs, at least seven Oscars, one Tony, and nine IJNAF Zeros carried out daylight attacks – all but four of the fighters fell to the guns of the 342nd Fighter Squadron for the loss of one P-47D and its pilot. The 1st

Battle of Cape Waios

To meet a Japanese destroyer force loaded with troops steaming to reinforce Biak, the 310th Bomb Wing at Wakde called on the 17th Reconnaissance Squadron's B-25Ds. On June 8, ten bombers, led by Major William Tennille, escorted by 17 475th Fighter Group P-38Js, found the Japanese convoy at 1250hrs about 40nm north of Cape Waios. The weather was clear and the B-25s evaded about ten Zero fighters from the 23rd Air Flotilla to make low-level attacks against the convoy, which consisted of six destroyers. Tennille and his wingman led the attack but 25mm antiaircraft fire from the destroyers shot down both aircraft. However, with the Japanese fighters occupied by the covering P-38s, the remaining B-25s managed to follow Tennille through the antiaircraft fire. *Harusame* suffered two direct bomb hits and sank; 74 of the crew were killed and another 11 were wounded, three other destroyers suffered light damage. The P-38s claimed three Zeros destroyed with one of their own crash landing at Wakde, while the destroyers shot down an additional B-25D and severely damaged the remaining seven. In total, 19 B-25 aircrew were killed. The convoy continued toward Biak but later turned back after meeting American destroyers. For his leadership, Tennille was posthumously awarded the Congressional Medal of Honor.

Jim Laurier

Air Fleet sent reinforcements to the 23rd Air Flotilla. The first batch included 70 fighters, four reconnaissance aircraft, and 16 dive-bombers. The next day, the Naval General Staff ordered another fifty aircraft from Japan and 40 more aircraft (20 fighters and 20 bombers) from the Marianas to move to New Guinea. As a result, the 23rd Air Flotilla's strength rose from 16 to some 200 aircraft. With this infusion of strength, renewed attacks were made on the beachhead on May 29–30. But after heavy losses, just 18 aircraft were left operational by May 30. Only harassing attacks were made until June 8. Beginning on May 31, another 166 IJNAF aircraft were ordered to transfer from the Marianas to Sorong on the northwest tip of New Guinea to conduct further attacks. The Allies, meanwhile, began a series of almost daily ground support attacks on IJA positions on Biak in a desperate, yet futile, attempt to seize Biak's airfields in time to use them to support POA's Central Pacific operations.

Despite the IGHQ stipulation that Biak was only to be held for as long as possible, this assessment was changed because the IJN was planning for the upcoming decisive battle (*A-Go*) in the general area of the Palau Islands. Given this, the Naval General Staff assessed that the retention of Biak's airfields was crucial to the IJN's ability to control the air over the decisive battle zone. On May 29, Southwest Area Fleet and Southern Army headquarters formulated Operation *Kon* to move reinforcements to Biak. The first attempt to land troops on Biak on June 4 was abandoned when a US carrier force was mistakenly reported nearby. The IJN relief force was also located and attacked by 63rd Bomb Squadron Snoopers just after midnight. The Japanese tried again on June 8. After surviving another 5th Air Force attack off Cape Waios, the reinforcement group turned back after encountering Allied naval forces.

Throughout the operation, the diminished skills of Japanese aviators were in evidence. On June 2, 54 23rd Air Flotilla aircraft attacked eight LSTs off Biak. In a 65-minute attack against these slow targets with no air cover, only a single ship suffered a near miss from a bomb. Twelve Japanese aircraft were lost. The following day another Allied convoy bound for Biak comprising three destroyers, eight LSTs, and four infantry landing craft was attacked by 32 Zeros and nine bombers from the 23rd Air Flotilla and ten IJAAF aircraft. For the loss of 11 aircraft, only light damage was inflicted on the American vessels. On June 4, a force of 28 fighters and nine bombers from the 23rd Air Flotilla caught the main Allied naval force in the area without air cover. Despite being vulnerable, only two light cruisers were slightly damaged by near misses that did not impair their fighting capabilities.

The Japanese cancelled *Kon* to challenge Nimitz's attacks in the Marianas on June 11. The 23rd Air Flotilla's remaining 150 aircraft left Sorong for the Palaus and flotilla headquarters left Sorong for Ambon on June 28. Abandoned by the IJN, and without effective IJAAF air support, the IJA Biak garrison was reduced to scattered groups of starving men by the end of June. The Americans placed Mokmer airfield into service on June 20. Work on an airfield on the island of Owi, three miles southeast of Biak, began on June 7 when it became clear Japanese resistance on Biak would upset Kenney's timetable. Owi airfield was usable from June 17.

The Allies devoted the remainder of June and July to preparing for the final push westward in New Guinea, supporting Allied ground forces fighting on Biak and Noemfoor, and battling 18th Army elements threatening Allied coastal positions. Airfields, maritime traffic, and other targets on Noemfoor, the Vogelkop Peninsula, and around Geelvink and Sekar Bays and MacCluer Gulf were daily targets of Allied air units. Noemfoor was assaulted on July 2 by the 158th Infantry Regimental Combat Team. The previous day, to prepare for the upcoming landing, 132 B-24s, B-25s, and A-20s had dropped 195 tons of bombs on IJA positions and P-38s had hit Kamiri and Kornasoren airfields with 11 tons of 1,000lb bombs. The landing itself was covered by the 8th, 348th, and 475th Fighter Groups and

The 82nd and 110th Tactical Reconnaissance Squadrons were the last SWPA units to fly the P-39. The 110th operated from Tadji from May 25, 1944, supporting RAAF No 71 Wing Beauforts and Beaufighters in ground attack missions. Here 110th pilots discuss a mission with RAAF Beaufort crews in front of a squadron P-39N. (AWM)

Nos 75 and 80 Squadron Kittyhawks, while 54 B-24s, B-25s, and A-20s hit Noemfoor's Kamiri, Kornasoren, and Namber airfields. The 421st Night Fighter Squadron's new P-61s covered the landing area at dawn and dusk. Noemfoor was secured by July 7. Kamiri was operational by July 18, and No 10 Operational Group, having moved from Aitape, took control of Kamiri where many RAAF units were based, while the 309th Bomb Wing was to control USAAF units based at Kornasoren.

As Biak, Noemfoor, and Owi began to fill up with Allied air units, the capstone to MacArthur's New Guinea campaign was the seizure of an airfield on the northwestern coast that Kenney earmarked for 13th Air Force units. Reconnaissance during June showed that the Mar–Sansapor area possessed good landing terrain with the possibility for airfield development. The Allies, however, did not follow their previous practice of softening-up strikes against the target area prior to the Mar–Sansapor landings. Rather, Whitehead directed attacks around western New Guinea and the NEI to seal off potential Japanese interference with the planned July 30–31 6th Infantry Division landings. Intelligence assessments gave the Japanese about 128 aircraft on Halmahera, so on July 27 Whitehead ordered an attack on Lolobata and Miti airfields by 28 22nd, 23 43rd, and 36 90th Bomb Group B-24s carrying 23lb fragmentation bombs. Meanwhile Galela was struck by 20 38th and 27 345th Bomb Group B-25s, escorted by 50 8th and 19 475th Fighter Group P-38s. The Japanese were again caught by surprise and air combat claims amounted to 15, some of which were caught taking off or landing. One 431st Squadron P-38 ditched due to mechanical trouble with the pilot being rescued. The bombers claimed at least 27 aircraft destroyed on the ground while suffering two B-24s and three B-25s damaged by antiaircraft fire. This attack and one the following day effectively closed out the Japanese air threat to New Guinea.

The landings at Mar and Middleburg Island on July 30 and at Sansapor on July 31 were unmolested by Japanese aircraft. MacArthur's troops had advanced 1,500 miles during the New Guinea campaign that was now concluded, and Kenney's FEAF were only 600 miles from the Philippines.

Kokas, a seaplane base with docks and supply storage, was targeted by 12 312th Bomb Group A-20Gs on July 22, 1944. This 387th Bomb Squadron A-20G, the only 312th aircraft lost in the attack, goes down after being hit by antiaircraft fire. Smoke rises from bomb explosions above the long-roofed building in the background. (NARA)

ANALYSIS AND CONCLUSION

The Allied perspective

Getting supplies to the Hollandia landing force by air was critical, due to inadequate trails from the beaches to the airfield objectives. Here a 433rd Troop Carrier Group C-47A, the first to land at the unrepaired Cyclops airstrip after its capture, rolls past the remains of a 63rd Air Regiment Oscar. (NARA)

Although the Allies faced significant problems in accumulating, maintaining, and managing their air assets throughout the campaign, the chief reason for their ultimate victory lay in their ability to respond to challenging circumstances both reasonably and flexibly. In this they were, of course, greatly aided by good intelligence from communications and photographic reconnaissance, but they also had the advantage of both the strategic and operational initiatives that allowed them to clearly visualize their objectives and thoroughly prepare for supporting air operations. They also successfully orchestrated their assets across the entire theater, with units in one area conducting operations that contributed to success elsewhere. In addition to the mutually supporting SWPA–SOPAC raids on Rabaul, strikes on IJAAF airfields on the New Guinea coast supported the New Britain Arawe and Cape Gloucester landings, and the operations flown from NWA, especially by the 380th Bomb Group, in no small measure harassed Japanese air and transport operations as well as directly supporting the Allied offensive operations from Hollandia on.

As in the earlier New Guinea campaign, the Allies continued to innovate to achieve the maximum results from their forces. The Nadzab drop was the only example in World War II of Allied use of paratroops in a strategic rather than in a tactical context, using them to seize a base from which to conduct future operations rather than just dropping them behind enemy lines for a vertical tactical envelopment. The flight paths taken during attacks on Rabaul and on Wewak's airfields were planned to avoid or suppress antiaircraft fire prior to low-level strikes, which were done to achieve the greatest accuracy. They also used a mix of bomb types, some developed in theater, to deal with various target types. Operationally, they figured out the best way to use air power to mitigate the real risks they faced in such cases as the Arawe, Cape Gloucester, Admiralties and Hollandia assaults, staging aircraft to maximize loiter time over the objectives and timing each squadron's part in the operation for maximum coverage. Although bad weather sometimes interfered with these carefully laid plans, they generally worked well. The Allies were also adept at concealing key capabilities

The 35th Fighter Squadron saw intense combat on December 26, 1943, at Cape Gloucester, where its P-40Ns sit in February 1944 on Marston matting with mud oozing through. The P-40/Kittyhawk units were usually the first to occupy unimproved, unrepaired, or new rough-hewn airfields because they could operate from them more easily than other fighter types. (NARA)

from the Japanese, such as Tsili Tsili and the extended-range P-38s, until they were ready to spring them on the unsuspecting IJAAF.

The numerous airstrips built or improved – from the large Nadzab and Gusap to the smaller Corunna Downs in Australia and Tsili Tsili and others in the New Guinea highlands – were a key to the Allied victory. The Allies employed sufficient manpower (including many local tribesmen) and equipment for this purpose. These airstrips provided the Allies with numerous places from which to stage and/or recover from long-range strikes and escorts and to conduct supply or tactical reconnaissance for the ground troops. The extensive use of auxiliary fuel tanks on both bombers and fighters was likewise essential for successful operations. For these reasons Kenney and Bostock achieved total air supremacy in little more than a year and were able to guarantee MacArthur's amphibious assaults sufficient cover from Japanese air attacks. The Allied air forces cooperated reasonably well with their naval and ground counterparts in the timing of attacks in conjunction with naval gunfire support or ground force moves against key objectives in the Huon Peninsula and Markham/Ramu Valley fighting.

The Japanese perspective

By May 1943, the Japanese position in their Southeast Area was precarious. Japanese forces were attempting to hold a front of approximately 1,200 miles from Lae and Salamaua in eastern New Guinea to the Central Solomons. Their forces were totally inadequate to cover such an extended front. Added to this was their initial misunderstanding that, in the case of New Guinea, their situation after their loss of Buna required a shift from offense to defense. Although they no longer held the operational initiative, IGHQ still issued instructions to their forces that focused on ultimately taking Port Moresby. Making their situation almost impossible was that the movement of reinforcements and supplies to critical points in this huge battle area had to be conducted in the face of growing Allied air and sea power.

Without achieving at least local air superiority for a given period of time, any Japanese operations in the Southeast Area were doomed to failure. During the New Guinea campaign, the lack of local air superiority severely limited Japanese effectiveness against Allied amphibious assaults and against key fixed targets – such as the airfields at Dobodura, Tsili Tsili, Nadzab, Gusap, and Saidor – and curtailed the support they could give to their own ground forces during the Huon Peninsula fighting.

There were several interrelated reasons for the ultimate Japanese defeat in the air campaign for New Guinea. Given a weak-to-nonexistent air warning system and highly vulnerable supply lines, the Japanese were severely handicapped in fighting the air war over New Guinea. The Japanese also failed to learn from their mistakes made during their 1942 New Guinea air campaign.

First of all, the Japanese failed to comprehend how to fight a prolonged air campaign against a modern opponent. Unlike the strategy employed by Kenney, Kusaka, Teramoto, and other Japanese air commanders conducted small attacks on a series of targets. Neither Teramoto nor Kusaka were able to plan and execute a sustained, positive application of air power due to poor situational awareness, insurmountable logistical problems, and poor intelligence, which did not allow them to identify the proper targets or locations of Allied attacks in time to make sufficient preparations or to respond adequately once the Allied objective was clear. To cite just one example, the stark difference in forces employed and outcomes between the IJAAF attacks on new Allied airfields in the New Guinea highlands beginning in June, leading up to the August 15, 1943, IJAAF attack on Tsili Tsili, and the Allied campaign against Wewak beginning with the August 17–18 USAAF attacks on Wewak's airfields perfectly exemplified how woefully incoherent the Japanese scheme of operations was compared to that of the Allies in a protracted air contest.

Throughout the campaign the IJAAF proved unable to adequately protect maritime supply traffic. Here an unidentified Oscar attacks one of 16 405th Bomb Squadron B-25Ds striking supply shipping off Wewak on September 2, 1943. The 405th lost two B-25s, but claimed six fighters destroyed and at least three damaged transports. (NARA)

Secondly, the IJAAF was unable to respond successfully to the series of swift and powerful Allied blows because it continuously suffered serious attrition. This meant that the stream of reinforcements poured into New Guinea were expended with little effect. Despite the almost continuous infusion of units and replacement aircraft, from the second half of 1943 the IJAAF faced a growing numerical disadvantage in the air. As the Allied air forces grew, the Japanese watched their air strength decline into irrelevance by the end of the campaign. For example, the IJAAF 14th Air Brigade's pairing of fighter regiments for operations in February 1944 was forced upon 4th Air Army due to the lack of serviceable aircraft. The Japanese were also unable to replace skilled pilots and ground staff lost. In particular, the quality of new pilots significantly declined during the course of the campaign. This is reflected not only in air combat results but in the fact that a fifth of IJAAF losses were "operational" - flying and landing accidents.

Thirdly, the Japanese also faced a growing technological disadvantage. Japanese aircraft were outmatched in all important performance areas, with the exception of fighters'

The IJAAF was consistently unable to defend its airfields, and over 50 percent of its aircraft losses during the campaign occurred on the ground. Here, parademos drift down on 75th Air Regiment Lilys at But during one of the several March 1944 5th Air Force Wewak-area raids. (NARA)

maneuverability. Japanese aircraft generally did not carry heavy armament and possessed only marginal ability to sustain damage. Their principal fighters, the Oscar and Zero, were obsolescent and markedly inferior in most respects to the more modern Allied fighters. For example, the only IJAAF weapons innovations, the upgrading of the wing armament in the later model Tonys to 20mm cannon in place of 12.7mm machine guns and the occasional use of aerial phosphorous bombs, made no discernable positive impact on the situation. Deployed in insufficient numbers, Japanese bombers were not good offensive platforms with their small bomb loads and weak defensive armament.

Finally, in the seemingly mundane area of airfield construction and protection, the Japanese suffered from crippling problems. Airfield construction was accomplished by manual labor, making progress difficult and time consuming. Aside from airstrips and taxiways, IJAAF airfields generally lacked adequate dispersal space, and the lack of adequate ground transportation meant that fuel and ammunition stores also could not be dispersed to relatively safe locations, but instead they had to be nearer the aircraft. Antiaircraft positions were frequently poorly sited and crews, often lacking forewarning, were unready to defend against the combination of both high- and low-altitude attacks Allied aircraft favored. IJAAF aircraft were thus continually caught in the open and destroyed. According to the estimate of one senior Japanese officer, over half of all IJAAF losses were suffered on the ground. In a war of attrition, which the New Guinea air campaign was, the Japanese had none of the ingredients for victory.

BIBLIOGRAPHY

Air Command and Staff College, *Airpower Employment of the Fifth Air Force in the World War II Southwest Pacific Theater*, Creative Space Publishers Platform, Middletown, DE (2014)

Barbey, Daniel E., *MacArthur's Amphibious Navy*, United States Naval Institute, Annapolis, MD (1969)

Bergerud, Eric M., *Fire in the Sky*, Westview Press, Boulder, CO (2000)

Birdsall, Steve, *Flying Buccaneers*, Doubleday and Co., Garden City, NY (1977)

Carter, Kit C., and Robert Mueller, *The Army Air Forces in World War II Combat Chronology 1941–1945*, Office of Air Force History, Washington, DC (1973)

Claringbould, Michael John, *Pacific Adversaries, Vol. 1*, Avonmore Books, Kent Town, Australia (2019)

Claringbould, Michael John, *Pacific Profiles, Vols 1, 2, 5, and 13*, Avonmore Books, Kent Town, Australia (2020–24)

Cooling, Benjamin (ed.), *Case Studies in the Achievement of Air Superiority*, Center for Air Force History, Washington, DC (1994)

Cooper, Anthony, *Darwin Spitfires*, New South, Sydney, Australia (2011)

Craven, W.F. and J.L. Cate, eds, *The Army Air Forces in World War II, Vol. IV: The Pacific – Guadalcanal to Saipan*, University of Chicago Press, Chicago, IL (1950)

Crocker, Mel, *Black Cats and Dumbos: WWII's Fighting PBYs*, TAB Books, Blue Ridge Summit, PA (1987)

Defense Research Institute War History Room, *Military History Series 22: Army Air Operations in Western New Guinea*, Defense Research Institute, Tokyo, Japan (n.d.)

Drea, Edward J., *MacArthur's ULTRA*, University Press of Kansas, Lawrence, KS (1992)

Fain, James E., Howard L. Bergman, Grant C. Cannon and Julian A. Riser, *The Flying Circus – 380th Bomb Group*, Commanday-Roth Company, New York, NY (1946)

Gaylor, Walter, Don L. Evans, Harry A. Nelson and Lawrence J. Hickey, *Revenge of the Red Raiders*, International Historical Research Associates, Boulder, CO (n.d.)

Griffith, Thomas E. Jr, *MacArthur's Airman*, University Press of Kansas, Lawrence, KS (1998)

Hata, Ikuhiko, Yasuho Izawa and Christopher Shores, *Japanese Army Air Force Fighter Units and Their Aces 1931–1945*, Grub Street, London, UK (2002)

Hata, Ikuhiko and Yasuho Izawa, *Japanese Naval Aces and Fighter Units in World War II*, Naval Institute Press, Annapolis, MD (1989)

Haugland, Vern, *The AAF against Japan*, Harper and Brothers, New York, NY (1948)

Headquarters, 38th Bomb Group (M) APO 337, *38th Bombardment Group (M) "Pacific Sun Setters" – 5th Air Force*, n.p., (1946)

Henebry, John P., *The Grim Reapers*, Pictorial Histories Publishing, Missoula, MT (2002)

Hewitt, J.E., *Adversity in Success*, Langate Publishing, South Yarra, Australia (1980)

Hickey, Lawrence J., *Warpath across the Pacific*, International Historical Research Associates, Boulder, CO (2008)

Hickey, Lawrence J., Michael H. Levy and Michael J. Claringbould, *Rampage of the Roarin' 20's*, International Historical Research Associates, Boulder, CO (2009)

Hickey, Lawrence J., James T. Pettus, Osamu Tagaya, Edward M. Rogers, Madison D. Jonas and Steve Birdsall, *Ken's Men against The Empire, Vols I and II*, International Historical Research Associates, Boulder, CO (2016, 2019)

Ichimura, Hiroshi, *Ki-43 'Oscar' Aces of World War 2*, Osprey Publishing, Botley (2009)

Janowicz, Krzysztof, *68 Sentai*, Kagero, Lublin, Poland (2003)

Japanese Demobilization Bureaux, *Reports of General MacArthur, Japanese Operations in the Southwest Pacific Area, Vol. II, Pt I*, Center for Military History, Washington, DC (1994)

Japanese Monograph No. 31, *Air Operations in the Southern Area, 1941–1945* (n.d.)

Japanese Monograph No. 32, *Southeast Area Air Operations Record Nov. 1942–Apr. 1944* (n.d.)

Japanese Monograph No. 140, *Outline of Southeast Area Air Operations, Part IV, July–November 1943* (n.d.)

Japanese Monograph No. 142, *Outline of Southeast Area Air Operations, Part V, Nov. 1943–May 1944* (n.d.)

Kenney, George C., *General Kenney Reports*, Office of Air Force History, Washington, DC (1987)

Kibo, Jiro, *Complete History of the Army Air Corps*, Asahi Sonorama, Tokyo, Japan (n.d.)

Kreis, John F., *Air Warfare and Air Base Air Defense 1914–1973*, Office of Air Force History, Washington, DC (1988)

Kreis, John F. (ed.) *Piercing the Fog*, Air Force History and Museums Program, Washington, DC (1996)

Lewis, Dr Tom, *Bombers North*, Avonmore Books, Kent Town, Australia (2023)

Lloyd, Alwyn T., *Liberator: America's Global Bomber*, Pictorial Histories Publishing Co., Missoula, MT (1993)

MacDonald, Rod, *Task Force 58*, Naval Institute Press, Annapolis, MD (2021)

McAulay, Lex, *MacArthur's Eagles: The US Air War over New Guinea, 1943–1944*, Naval Institute Press, Annapolis, MD (2005)

Mikesh, Robert C. and Osamu Tagaya, *Moonlight Interceptor*, Smithsonian Institution Press, Washington, DC (1985)

Miller, John, *Cartwheel: The Reduction of Rabaul*, Center of Military History, United States Army, Washington, DC (1990)

Millman, Nicholas, *Ki-61 and Ki-100 Aces*, Osprey Publishing, Botley, UK (2015)

Odgers, George, *Air War against Japan 1943–1945*, Australian War Memorial, Canberra, Australia (1968)

Paduch, Dariusz, *Japanese Heavy Fighters 1937–1945*, Kagero, Lublin, Poland (2022)

Perrone, Stephen P., *World War II B-24 "Snoopers,"* NJSG, Somerdale, NJ (2003)

Rust, Kenn C., *Fifth Air Force Story*, Historical Aviation Album, Temple City, CA (1973)

Rust, Kenn C. and Dana Bell, *Thirteenth Air Force Story*, Historical Aviation Album, Temple City, CA (1981)

Shindo, Hiroyuki, *Japanese Air Operations over New Guinea during the Second World War*, Journal of the Australian War Memorial, No. 34, Canberra, Australia (2001)

Smith, Robert Ross, *The Approach to the Philippines*, Center of Military History, Unted States Army, Washington, DC (1984)

United States Strategic Bombing Survey, *The Fifth Air Force in the War against Japan*, Alpha Editions, n.p. (2020)

United States Strategic Bombing Survey, *Interrogations of Japanese Officials Vols 1 and 2*, Skilled Books, India (n.d.)

War History Office, *War History Series: Western New Guinea Area Army and Air Operations*, National Defense Agency Defense Research Institute, Tokyo, Japan (n.d.)

Watson, Richard L., *The Fifth Air Force in the Huon Peninsula Campaign January to October 1943*, Army Air Forces Historical Office, Washington, DC (1946)

Wolf, William, *The 5th Fighter Command in World War II, Vols 1 and 2*, Schiffer Military History, Atglen, PA (2011, 2012)

Woods, Wiley O., *Legacy of the 90th Bombardment Group*, Turner Publishing, Paducah, KY (1994)

INDEX